Memoirs of a Reluctant Gunner
Vincent Gilbert

Written by Vincent Gilbert

Cover image by Gordon Wilberforce

ISBN: {hbk) 978-1-928171-22-5
ISBN: (pbk) 978-1-928171-23-2
ISBN: (ebk) 978-1-928171-24-9

Vocamus Community Publications
130 Dublin Street North
Guelph, Ontario
N1H 4N4

www.vocamus.net

To my wife Kathleen
and to my childhood friend Eric Mansell

Acknowledgements

Thanks to Jeremy Luke Hill, for his advice and for bringing it all together, and to Gordon Wilberforce, for the book cover.

Table of Contents

Foreword

World War II was a terrible waste of life. Over 52 million people lost their lives in the conflict. Some died fighting for what they believed to be a righteous cause, while patriots and, what the Germans called 'inferior human beings', were tortured and murdered in the most brutal fashion. Thousands of others died sleeping in their beds or sheltering in underground bunkers.

Hitler and the whole German race have much to answer for. Millions of men, women and children were transported like cattle across Europe to death camps with names like Buchenfeld, Auschwitz and Belson, and yet a huge percentage of the German people denied any knowledge of these atrocities. One has only to watch newsreels of their triumphant Fuhrer parading through Berlin after his victories in Austria, Poland, France, and the many other countries they marched into, to see how much the German population supported him and his sadistic henchmen, evidence that cannot be denied.

In time, the world may pardon the 'Huns', but I will never forgive them. My only hope is that future generations will not forget the misery and havoc this 'Master Race' brought upon the world.

The German forces caused massive destruction in the countries that came under their jackboots. Cities such as Rotterdam, Warsaw, Leningrad, Stalingrad, Belgrade, Kiev, London and Coventry were devastated, and yet the Germans still have the audacity to complain about the Allies obliterating Dresden, Berlin and Hamburg. The

German Gestapo and SS Troops, in some cases, destroyed whole towns and villages including the people who lived there. They just had to be stopped.

Our awe-inspiring wartime Prime Minister, Winston Churchill, just about had it right when he said, "The German nation is either at your throat or at your feet." What would Britain, or the world for that matter, have done without that great leader, especially when our small island stood alone for more than a year. Although I have never voted for his political party, I truly believe that he is the greatest Englishman, and perhaps the greatest English speaking man, of all time. Today, no one ever thinks about what conditions would have been like in Britain, Europe, or even the world, if Winston Spencer Churchill had not lived.

May I remind the reader, that after the miraculous retreat from Dunkirk, some in the British Cabinet were all for seeking a peace treaty with the Nazis, but in Churchill's first speech as Prime Minister, he made it perfectly clear to the whole world, that Britain would fight on alone until the bitter end. Those of us who listened to that broadcast will never forget his closing words. "We shall fight in the hills, we shall fight no matter the cost. We shall never surrender."

This is the story of one individual's experience during that conflict. It is Vinnie Gilbert's story. The army changed my whole life, and was a positive, negative, and at times a horrible experience. A brave person I most certainly am not. A little adventuresome perhaps, but as fate would have it, I did not see action on the battlefield, although I was machine gunned from the air, spent many nights when bombs were falling all around, and did get wounded as a result of "friendly fire".

The reader should understand the reason why for being made aware of the above. It is because the honour for winning the war must go to those who fought, died, or were terribly wounded, both mentally and physically, and not to gunners like me, who through some twist of fate, ended the war sitting behind a desk. They are the heroes. They are the ones to whom the world should be forever indebted.

I did not suffer the terrible battering of those valiant troops struggling to get off the beaches of Dunkirk, or slash my way through the jungles of Burma, or endure the perils of Atlantic and North Sea convoys. I did not suffer the slogging back and forth battles in the

Western Desert in North Africa, or brave the bullets and shells on "D" Day, or endure the appalling and vicious cruelty of the Japanese prisoner of war camps.

No, I was one of the lucky ones.

I have tried to make this narrative as light hearted as possible, but how can one be light hearted about one's friends being killed or terribly wounded. Their names will be forever tucked away in a sad and special place in my memory.

Vincent F. Gilbert

September 2, 2015

Chapter One
Copthorne Barracks, Shrewsbury

As I recall, it was in October 1943, when the letter arrived from His Majesty King George VI, extending an invitation to assist him in the conduct of the war. It went something like this:—

Dear Vinnie, [He always called me Vinnie]

Liz, myself and the kids are fine, but that`s not really what I want to talk to you about. The war, as you know, is not going too well, so Mr. Churchill and I thought it a good idea to inquire if you would like to help out by joining the army? A very nice welcoming reception has been arranged for you at Copthorne Barracks in Shrewsbury, so if you can spare the time perhaps you could attend before 12:00 hours on 16 Oct. 1943.

See you soon.

George and Winston.

P.S. If you don't accept our invitation, we will send two damn great military policemen to come and get you.

How could one refuse such a regal request?

I must confess that the letter did not actually come from King George VI, but came via the War Office, and went something like,

In accordance with the War Measures Act you are hereby ordered to report for military duty at Copthorne Barracks, Shrewsbury, in the county of Shropshire by 12:00 hours on 16 October 1943. Blah, blah, blah.

On the following Friday afternoon, after collecting what little wages were owing to Gilbert [Clock No. 09/033], I said a not so sad farewell to the English Electric Co. Ltd., for to be honest, a large part of me was glad to be getting away from tedious factory life. On that same evening, I visited my music teacher, Dr. Mathews, and informed him that I would not be continuing my studies as I had been called upon to serve king and country. Only the week before I had paid him two guineas for my next 10 lessons, an enormous sum when one realizes I was only earning about 16 shillings per week. At the end of the hour's tuition, we shook hands and he wished me, "All the best". He then returned the whole of my two guineas saying, "Come back and see me when the war is over". To my everlasting regret, I never did.

I cannot remember much about the following days, except that one of the first things I did was write to my best friend, Private Eric Mansell, 14654727, of the 1st battalion, South Lancashire Regiment. The rest of the time was spent calling on, and saying goodbye to friends.

On Tuesday evening I said goodbye to my sister May and her husband Eric. Next came my eldest brother Horace and his wife Joan, who imparted much advice about behaving myself, being careful with whom I mixed, and the hygienic use of toilet seats. Then at 6:00 o'clock the following morning, after many hugs, kisses and tears from my mother, father and brother Tom, I picked up the small suitcase containing such things as tooth brush, underwear, pajamas etc., and set off for Stafford railway station. Brother Jack, who happened to be a driver on the LMS railway [a reserved occupation], accompanied me, but hardly said a word. He knew exactly which train to catch and the platform from where it would leave. After seeing me to a compartment, he gave his little brother a big hug, turned on his heels and quickly walked away. There were tears in his eyes.

My own feelings were mixed. It was the start of a great adventure into the unknown, were there would be strict discipline, hard training, people to meet very much different from my hometown friends, danger, death and destruction. I would also be seeing sights and places only previously seen on the silver screen, or read about in books. It was, above all, the beginning of a much needed education into the ways of the world.

There was, however, one thing in particular that gave me great cause for concern, and try as I might, it would not retreat from my thoughts. Would I have to kill someone? How could anyone with an ounce of compassion kill a complete stranger, a fellow human being, and live with himself afterwards? Would I be able to do it? Up until now, the most lethal thing I had wielded was an axe, and that had only been used to chop firewood. I had never handled a gun in my life, and yet here I was embarking on a journey that would see me firing a rifle, machine gun, mortar, and a large piece of artillery. In addition, it was the first time in my life I had been away from home completely on my own. No trusty pals or family to keep me company and confide in. I was young, naive, fearful, insecure, and extremely apprehensive. I sat in the carriage, cold and alone.

At long last, the Guard blew his whistle, a flag was waved, the engine gave a great belch of steam, the train began to move, and Stafford, the town I had called home for 18 years was gradually left behind. Venable's timber yard, Bagnall's locomotive works, Universal Grinding Wheel Co., and finally the castle drifted slowly by. Factories and rows of houses gave way to woods, fields, thatched cottages, and the occasional farm. As the train clackerty-clacked westwards, stops were made at numerous villages, and at each station one or two people clad in heavy overcoats clambered on board, while milk churns were noisily loaded into a wagon to the rear. After the town of Wellington, the Wrekin, that strange cone shaped hill came into view, and then it too gradually disappeared in the early morning mist. Actually, the countryside between the two county towns of Stafford and Shrewsbury is really quite attractive. However, on this particular morning, sitting in that cold, dank carriage, peering through the drizzle, mist, and at times, thick fog made it a miserable yet memorable journey.

When the train eventually puffed its way into Shrewsbury station, the only people around were a few commuters, railway personnel, and a couple of hefty military policemen, known in the forces as "Red Caps" because of the red band around their hats. "Are you lost son?" said one of them as I approached. "Son" indeed. Didn't they realize they were looking at a future 5 feet 5 inches 100 lbs. Commando? The problem was I only looked about 14 years old, so there was an excuse for them.

"Yes," I replied, "I have to report to Copthorne Barracks by 12 o'clock."

He stared at me for a few seconds, made some remark to his fellow M.P. about cradle snatching, and then, placing his hand on my shoulder, advised me, "Stand over by that bus stop and catch the number 23 bus. It will drop you right outside the gate." So I did, and so did the bus.

On the right, just inside the gate, was the Guard Room, but it was the spectacle taking place straight ahead on the Barrack Square that made my kneecaps rattle and my hair stand on end. Light infantry do not march like ordinary infantry soldiers, but perform practically everything at the double, and these poor blighters on the parade ground were being drilled in full battle order. If ever there was a time when I thought about informing his majesty about what to do with his invitation, this was it.

Copthorne Barracks is the home depot of the King's Own Shropshire Light Infantry [the KSLI], and the sight that greeted this new recruit as he walked through those hallowed gates put the fear of God into him, but as the reader will learn, it was only the first of many shocks to be absorbed on that never to be forgotten October day.

"You there, are you reporting for duty?" shouted a voice that would have been better employed as a fog signal on Beachy Head.

"Yes," the Gilbert replied.

"Yes sergeant," the voice snapped back, pointing to three stripes on his arm.

"Yes sergeant," I replied.

"Are you reporting for duty?" he repeated.

Again I replied, "Yes sergeant."

"Go into the office, place your signature opposite your name on the list, and someone will give you further instructions," he ordered, pointing in the direction of what I learned later was, in fact, the Guardroom.

And so it was all that day. From this place to that place, signing dozens of bits of paper, listening to all sorts of short lectures, delivered so fast one could not take it all in. King's Regulation this and King's Regulation that. I hadn't a clue what they were talking about.

First stop was for a sort of medical examination. This consisted of being measured, weighed, reading a chart on the wall, a doctor who listened to your heart and asked a few questions, like "Can you breath?" and if the answer was in the affirmative, you were declared, "Fit for active service." Someone dressed as a soldier said, "Sign here and report over there," pointing to "there".

At "there" I joined two other recruits, and within a couple of minutes we three were directed to the Quarter Master's Store where we were issued with blankets, [no sheets], towels, socks, shirts [without collars], underwear, and a roll up pouch, [commonly known as a 'Housewife'] containing buttons, cotton, needles, thread, wool, patches, all "soldiers for the use of".

After the inevitable "Sign here", and loaded down with all this equipment, [by then we were a group of five], a corporal pointed to a building on the opposite side of the barrack square and told us, "That will be your billet for the rest of your stay here. Report to Corporal Abbot, and return here as soon as possible to collect your uniforms."

Unfortunately, here is where we made our first big mistake.

With our precious possessions, we strode forth onto and across the Parade Ground. About half way across, a klaxon of a voice blared out, "Where the bloody hell do you think you lot are going?" We didn't know whether this rude, uncouth person was referring to us or not, so we took another few steps before turning towards the voice. There, about thirty yards away, stood the daunting figure of the Regimental Sergeant Major in all his glory.

"Get off this bloody parade ground you horrible little men," the klaxon instructed us, "and never, ever walk across this square again. If you want to get from A to B, you walk around the square. Do you understand?" As the voice shouted, "A", a stick flashed from under his arm pointing to one side of the Parade Ground, and then to the opposite side when "B" was blasted out.

"Okay," we replied, which for some reason appeared to upset him. His face turned a sort of purple-orange colour, and vapor, similar to steam, issued from the top of his cap.

"YES SIR!" blasted out this human Tanoy. "And stand to attention when you talk to me," pointing to something on his wrist that resembled the lid off a tin of salmon. "I am the Regimental Sergeant Major of this regiment, and I will be keeping a bloody eye on you lot. Now bugger off." With that, he whipped his cane under his arm at exactly 90 degrees to his ramrod straight body, executed a perfect military style, foot slamming "about turn" and continued bellowing orders at the PBIs being drilled. "PBI" is army jargon for "Poor bloody infantry". Can't remember his name, but I will never forget that voice, or that face, a face only a mother could love.

We scuttled across that sacrosanct square, entered the designated building, where we were shown upstairs and told to pick out a bunk, starting at the far end of the room. There were two rows of wooden bunk beds, enough for about 40 bodies, and as first arrivals, we all chose top beds. The place was spotlessly clean, with a highly polished floor, and a small metal locker adjacent to each bed. We dumped our newly gained gear on the chosen bed, then promptly returned to the QM's store, this time by walking around the barrack square.

Back at the store, we were handed two huge indigestible sandwiches of cheese, and a large mug of tepid grey-brown liquid known as NAAFI "tea". [NAAFI stands for "Navy, Army and Air Force Institute".] Then, after having rid ourselves of this sumptuous repast, we were ordered to "Line up outside that door."

"That door" led into a large warehouse, and it was here that uniforms and boots were issued. To say that I was overwhelmed by the two Battle Dresses and fatigue uniform issued to me is putting it mildly, for surely they must have been made for a 300 lb., six feet twelve inches tall Goliath, with a chest to match. When attired I looked like one of Walt Disney's cartoon characters. Naturally, I pointed this out to the sergeant, to which he replied, "Where the hell do you think this is — Saville Row?'

Boots were a different kettle of fish. The utmost care was taken to see they fitted correctly with the advice to administer plenty of dubbing and then to polish same until one could see one's face in the toe cap. Asked where one collected the tins of dubbing and shoe polish, the same sergeant stated rather emphatically, that these items could be purchased from the NAAFI. This, before the army had even given us any money, and when pay did arrive, it amounted to the princely sum of 15 shillings and 6 pence per week, [Roughly $2.00 Canadian]. Luckily, I had brought a pound with me, but others had only 2 or 3 shillings in their pockets.

That evening, around five o'clock, our now large group, still in civilian clothes, but with our eating utensils, [soldiers for the use of], were taken to the mess hall for the evening meal. As we entered, a great roar went up with cries of, "Welcome to the Ritz" and "Does your mother know you're here?" plus other comical remarks. We lined up, collected our plates, and as we approached the servers our attention was drawn to a large notice threatening dire consequences to anyone wasting food, and reminding the recipients that men were risking and losing their lives transporting these provisions across the Atlantic Ocean. My thoughts immediately went out to my friends Lol Dowd and Ron Eley who were on North Atlantic convoy escort duty. Lol was on HMS Mounsey, and Ron on HMS Bentinck.

Returning to our luxurious accommodation, the new recruits put on their new uniforms, and tried to see how to make them fit a little better, but met with little success. By 9.30, most of the barrack room had made their beds and were fast asleep, thoroughly worn out.

Tomorrow was another day, and that started by the troops being rudely awakened at the unearthly hour of 6:00 A.M. by a bugle call, and cries of "Wakey wakey" and "Show a leg there" from the Orderly Sergeant. Copthorne was the only place in my military career where bugle calls still notified one of the times of day *i.e.* Reveille and Lights Out.

At 6:50 AM, the whole barrack room assembled outside, and marched off to the mess hall. It seems to be an inherent tradition among soldiers to complain about army cooking, but the meals here were better than I expected. Breakfast consisted of a great dollop of porridge, scrambled egg, some sort of sausage, bread, margarine, jam, and tea. Alas, not all postings were as well-appointed, as I would find out in the months ahead.

Back at our billet, we gathered around to be instructed on the correct KSLI way to fold blankets and lay out other accoutrement on the bed, ready for inspection. All beds and equipment had to line up from one end of the room to the other. Spare boots must be placed soles upward in order that the inspecting NCO or officer could determine if they were being worn every other day. Also, we were informed, a roster had been pinned to the notice board indicating who cleaned what, on which day. It was obvious the NCO in charge had performed this ritual many times before. It seemed we lucky people would be here for 6 weeks intensive primary training, after which we would be assigned to our different regiments or corps. Finally, we were told that when a private addresses an officer or NCO, or vice versa, he must always stand to attention, and that included Corporal Abbot.

At precisely 10:30 we stepped out upon that sacred Parade Ground to be shown the correct way to "Stand to attention", "Stand at ease", "Right dress", "About turn", "Right turn", "Halt", and, of course, march, all the time shouting "1, 2, 3, 1". Feet placed at 60 degrees, stomach in, chest out, chin in, shoulders back, head upright, eyes looking straight ahead, hands clenched with thumbs pointing down the seam of the trouser leg.

Berets were a big problem, because in most cases they just did not fit. A few times I thought I had gone blind, but luckily it was only that the beret had fallen over my eyes. The suggestion was made that we soak the band in water and let it dry overnight. The shrinkage was not enough in my case, so a big tuck had to be applied.

After lunch, this over-sized platoon marched over to the Armoury where, one by one we were called to a table, presented with a little brown book and asked to "Sign here". This little book we were informed was an Army Pay Book, commonly referred to as an "AB64", and upon opening it, I discovered I was now officially Private Gilbert, No 14856524, of the General Service Corps, another name for basic training battalions. This plain looking AB64 contained such information as your present unit, date of enlistment, rank, etc., a document, that must be carried at all times, and produced for identification when requested by authorized personnel, such as an officer or military policemen. To lose one's AB64 was most serious, and a chargeable offense under King's Regulations.

Next, the recruits accepted with open arms a small pack, large pack, ammunition pouches, webbing belt, tin hat, gas mask, gas cape, gaiters, field dressing, groundsheet, canteen, and mess tins, and ordered to "Sign here". After taking these items back to the billet, we returned once again, to be presented with such lovely articles as a Lee Enfield 303 rifle, bayonet, some bits of flannel, a small tubular weight on a 3 feet length of chord, and a tiny phial of light oil, followed by yet another "Sign here". Years later, I discovered that this famous rifle had been designed by a Mr. Lee who lived in Cambridge, Ontario, Canada, and was manufactured at a factory in Enfield, England. Hence, "Lee-Enfield".

We were not informed just what the above last three items were for, but we were instructed to "familiarize yourself with the weapon, and clean same ready for inspection tomorrow morning". Most of the occupants of the barrack room had no idea what they were supposed to do with all these bits and pieces, so we just watched the one or two others who did. Corporal Abbot was conspicuous by his absence. We removed the "bolt", placed a piece of flannel in the loop at the end of the cord, threaded the weight through the barrel and pulled the same through the bore. Obviously, the only name for this bit of gear was the "Pull Through". After passing another lightly oiled flannel through the barrel, all was packed away in a compartment concealed in the stock of the rifle.

Next morning, on the square, we formed three ranks and were instructed on how to "Open order — March". This is where the centre rank stands still, while the front and rear ranks take two paces away from them. The new recruits were then shown how to present the rifle for inspection, by extending the rifle forward at 45 degrees, pulling the trigger, releasing the bolt, and placing one's thumbnail at the magazine end of the bore.

The inspecting sergeant strolled along each rank, making derogatory remarks and declaring his disgust. Some he said had cobwebs in the bore; others had enough dirt to grow carrots. "These weapons," he declared, "may someday save your lives, and they will not do so in their present filthy condition. They will be inspected again after lunch when I expect them to be in pristine condition. When I look down that barrel, I want to be blinded by the reflection of the sun from your thumbnail. Do you understand?" Only trouble was, the weatherman had not ordered the sun to make an appearance on that cloud heavy day.

No one said a word.

"Do you understand?" he repeated loudly, and we all replied, "Yes Sergeant."

"Stand to attention when you speak to me," he bellowed out. "Now, once again, do you understand?" and bringing our feet together we all declared, "Yes Sergeant."

This performance completed, the following inspection was more personal. Some were criticized for not having clean webbing belts, even though these had only been issued the day before. Others for not having a good enough shave. [In those days, I only shaved once every three days.] The sergeant stood behind one unsuspecting recruit and inquired, "Am I hurting you private?"

"No Sergeant," came the reply.

"Well I damn well ought to be, because I'm standing on your hair. See that you get a bloody haircut today, and that applies to all of you. Do you understand?"

Feet together, "Yes sergeant."

"Over the weekend, your webbing belt, small and large packs, plus your ammunition pouches, will be cleaned and blanco'd ready for inspection on Monday morning. Brasses will also be highly polished," he announced. "Khaki coloured Blanco and Brasso is obtainable from the NAAFI, and if you don't know how to blanco your gear, ask the Barrack Room NCO. Is all that clearly understood?"

"Yes Sergeant," the lads replied in unison.

The expense did not stop with buying Blanco and Brasso. To apply the Blanco a small brush was required. Yet another very important requisite was a brass strip, about 8 inches by 2 inches, with a 1/8 slot 75% along the middle, plus yet another small brush and polishing duster. The brass strip, by sliding behind the brass buttons and up the slot, protected your greatcoat from being stained by the polish. I think it was called a Button Stick.

Saturday and Sunday was a time to get to know the other inmates and explore the barracks and Shrewsbury. The recruits were a very mixed bunch indeed. Most were nice fellows, but there were a couple of very unsavory characters.

The barracks, built in the early part of Queen Victoria's reign, can only be described as stark and grim. Believe me, it was a lovely feeling to walk out of those gates into the "fresh air". However, before venturing out, one had to visit the Guardroom to be inspected. It was ridiculous! How could anyone look smart when the uniform made one look like a sack of potatoes?

Shrewsbury is a friendly, hilly, pretty, historic, and interesting town that I would have liked to explore more, but alas, within a couple of weeks Private Gilbert 524 would find himself sitting on a train, bound for the south western outskirts of London.

The following week was engaged in taking various aptitude tests, filling in more forms, exercising in the gym, and drill on the Barrack Square. Some of these tests consisted of running around a room taking things out of a box and placing them in a pattern at the other end of the room. Some forms had puzzles to solve, whilst on others they wanted to know what we did in civilian life, what our hobbies were, and what organizations we belonged to etc. This questionnaire was so that the army could place a soldier where he would be the least effective. *i.e.* a baker in civilian life would obviously land up in the Tank Corps, and a lorry driver in the Army Catering Corps.

Ah! But little did we know that on the following Friday we would be invited to attend yet another of those delightful, "so called" medicals, and henceforth, all medicals on Fridays would be viewed with trepidation. On that particular afternoon, the platoon paraded outside in PT kit, and marched off in the direction of the Sick Bay. The large Nissen hut we approached had a central passageway with offices on either side. Orders were given to place our hands on our hips and proceed along the passageway in single file. Standing in a doorway, half way along, stood four medical orderlies, two on either side. On reaching these doorways, one orderly rubbed the arm with cotton wool soaked in antiseptic, and then the other orderly would jab in a syringe needle. These inoculations, [TT and TAB whatever that means], took place, one in each arm at roughly the same time. To say the recruits were taken completely by surprise is putting it mildly. A couple of chaps fainted, but there was yet another shock in store.

Turning left into the next office Private Gilbert was confronted by a doctor – a very attractive lady doctor. I looked at her dumbfounded; she looked at me with a sweet smile on her face.

"Drop them," she said, pointing at my shorts.

I hesitated. She did not. "Drop them, drop them," she ordered in a very authoritative voice, and began to pull my shorts down below my knees. She then began to handle me where no one had handled me since I was a very small boy. I thought, the army isn't so bad after all, but it would have been much nicer if all the other people had not been there, observing, grinning, and taking notes. Why were they taking notes?

"Cough," she said. I coughed. "Cough harder," she barked, and I complied. "Let me see your fingers," the command came, and a few seconds later, with my hastily brought up shorts in place, I was once again pronounced, "Fit for active service".

This latter inspection is known in the forces as an FFI [Free from Infection or Short Arms Inspection], and because these examinations are performed on a regular basis, I could look forward to dropping my pants many many times over the next few years. Ah, the things one must endure for king and country!

Many of the recruits spent the weekend nursing swollen and sore arms.

Mine were not too bad, so it didn't stop me from venturing out to explore the town once more. Shrewsbury is uniquely situated in a great "Ox bow" of the River Severn. To enter the town from the east, one crossed over The English Bridge, and, traveling west, left the town by passing over The Welsh Bridge. In recent years, Shrewsbury has been made even more famous by the Brother Caedfell mystery stories.

At roll call on the following Monday I was summoned to the company office. Next morning, I was informed that I would return blankets etc. to the QM's store, pack all my equipment, and report back to the office by 0900 hours. At that time, travel documents would be issued allowing me to travel to the barracks of the East Surrey Regiment at Kingston on Thames in Surrey.

What was going on? If I was joining the East Surrey's what about my basic training? Were they light infantry? Where exactly was Kingston on Thames? Was it in the thick of the bombing? Lots of questions, but no answers. However, in two days time, in the illustrious words of Sherlock Holmes, "All would be revealed."

It transpired that there were two of us bound for this suburb of London. David Webb, for that was the other fellow's name, was a farmer's son, who had spent all his life at Ashford Court Farm, Ludlow, in Shropshire. He was a chubby sort of fellow, with a cherubic smile. Unsure and hesitant as I was, David was so innocent and naïve it was hard to believe. The furthest he had ever traveled from Ludlow, was Ludlow. Over the next 16 weeks, Dave and I became close buddies, but at the end of that time, sadly we were posted to different regiments.

On Tuesday morning, Dave and I reported to the company office, and collected our travel documents, which stated emphatically,

> *You will proceed to Kingston Barracks by 1600 hours on that day,*
> *via Euston station, where you will report to the Railway Transport*
> *Officer [RTO] for further instructions.*

Within five minutes, a lorry was hurrying two mystified "soldiers" down to the railway station. There, the RTO looked over our bits of paper, stamped and signed same, and told us to catch the London train that would shortly be leaving platform 5.

So began our journey.

Chapter Two
Kingston on Thames

———⟨≡≡≡⟩———

The train was 80% full, and the stuffy, dirty carriages reeked of tobacco and human kind. We did manage to find seats, but alas there was nowhere to store our equipment. There was a luggage rack, but this was already loaded down. Our dilemma was resolved by squeezing our small and large backpacks under the seat and standing our kitbags and rifle between our legs. Not very comfortable for such a long journey, but it was the best we could do. This completed, we settled down to watch the passing parade, and although it was cold, the Shropshire countryside looked as beautiful as ever under its canopy of hoar frost.

On the outskirts of Wolverhampton, the bomb damage did not appear to be too bad, but as we progressed further into that part of the industrial midlands commonly known as "the black country", the devastation was very extensive. Whole streets had been demolished. At times, the train slowed down to a crawl where the bomb-damaged track was being repaired, an exercise repeated several times that day. Stops at Birmingham and Rugby allowed passengers to get off and even more to squeeze their way on board. Sardines had nothing on this. Not only were the corridors crowded, but people were also standing between the seats in the carriages. If one needed the toilet, it was just too bad.

Because of the invasion scare after the remnants of the allied forces had been evacuated from Dunkirk, all place names, signposts, in fact any notice board where the town's name was mentioned had been removed, so unless one was familiar with the region, one was completely lost. Those who were not familiar with Great Britain could quite possibly have believed the little town they were now passing through was named "Players Navy Cut", or

"Ladies Waiting Room", or "Guinness Is Good For You". Fortunately, there was always someone who would remark, "I guess this must be Rugby" or whatever town it was, and this would be confirmed by a porter striding up and down the platform shouting out the name.

The scene on the train was quite amazing. Since Dunkirk, the United Kingdom had become one gigantic island fortress, manned by soldiers, sailors, and airmen, plus their female counterparts, from all over the world, in addition to the thousands of refugees who had escaped from Nazi oppression. On this and all trains, it was commonplace for servicemen and women to far outnumber civilian passengers.

Looking out the window onto the platform, we could see men in uniform, saying a fond farewell to their sweethearts or wives. Some embraced while holding a small baby between them, as though they would never see or hold each other again, which of course, many thousands never did.

Onward the bursting-at-the-seams train steadily progressed, making its stop and go journey down the centre of "this sceptred isle", until the suburbs of London started to pass by. The time taken for this roughly 140 mile journey was four to five hours, and the quality of the carriage air was getting worse and worse. God help anyone who was claustrophobic.

Once again, the first bomb damage we witnessed did not appear too bad, but as we neared the centre of this great metropolis, the destruction was something to behold. Whole areas had been completely obliterated, as if some gigantic sword had taken a great swath through the landscape. Factories, houses, churches, and large office blocks had been wiped off the face of the earth. One hideous panorama was of a large cemetery, across which a stick of bombs had fallen. Bits of coffins and those who had occupied the graves were scattered all over the place. How would they clean up that grotesque scene, and who would perform the horrendous task? It reminded me of Coventry after it had been "blitzed" for three consecutive nights. Thousands of people had been killed in those raids, and no doubt some were still buried under the rubble. It was more of a shock for Dave than myself, for I had witnessed the destruction of Coventry.

Only twice in my lifetime had I visited the capitol city. Once on a day excursion with the school, [cost seven shillings and sixpence], and once when I was ten years old, when my older brother Jack took me for the day on a special railway pass, [he was an LMS railway employee], so the spectacle of all this desolation was quite overwhelming. I couldn't help thinking, "How can we possibly win this war, when the Germans are wiping out our cities like this?" but circumstances had changed since 1940-41, when Britain stood alone for over a year and had little with which to defend itself. That was the year Churchill told the British people, "The Battle of France is over, the Battle of Britain is about to begin. Therefore let us brace ourselves for the coming invasion, so that if the British empire and commonwealth shall last for a thousand years, people will look back and say, this was their finest hour."

The RTO at Euston Station looked at our documents, stamped same, then presented David and I with tickets for the "tube", [underground rail system], with instructions to report to the RTO at Waterloo Station. Euston was a mess, but Waterloo was even worse, with great holes in its roof and rubble all over the place. And yet people just took it as just another normal day, walking past girders dropping down from the roof and circling around bomb craters in the reception areas.

Down into the bowels of the earth Dave and I descended, and the sight of all those bunk beds, mattresses, and few precious personal possessions strewn out along the "tube" station platforms really brought home the hardships Londoners were coping with. Night after terrible night these brave people came down here to sleep and shelter from the bombs. Next morning they would ascend into the daylight, make their way through and around the terrible carnage in the streets, not knowing if their homes would still be there. If their dwelling had survived the night's raid, they would wash, [if there was water], have some breakfast, and off they would go to work in the factories and offices until it was time to descend into their subterranean "bedrooms" once more. This was the sort of courage that saw Britain through those terribly anxious times. A slogan on the wall proclaimed, "London can take it," — but for how long I wondered?

Although the "tube" stations were regarded as 100% safe, the Germans did have one "lucky" strike, when a bomb actually drifted into the street entrance of one station and down towards the platforms beneath before exploding, causing heavy casualties. Mile End Road I think it was.

Struggling through the heavy damage at Waterloo Station, we managed to find the RTO, who issued yet another railway ticket for Kingston on Thames. Here, together with others, we crowded aboard a waiting lorry and proceeded to our final destination. En route, again, there was much damage. Great piles of rubble where nice houses had once stood. The strange thing was how quickly one got used to this sort of thing.

And so we arrived at our mysterious new home. What a difference from Copthorne! The place seemed more relaxed, more pleasant, and yet one felt that discipline was just as strict. That sounds contradictory I know, but this was the initial impression. There was the usual Guardroom and Parade

Ground, but the people on duty treated these new arrivals in a gentler, more humane fashion.

A sergeant was drilling some troops on the parade ground, but at a more civilized pace than the KSLI, while around the square groups of young men dressed in PT gear were running around, then stopping to perform exercises, before racing off again. Who knows, perhaps I was going to be a 100-lb 5' 5" commando after all.

Documents duly exchanged, we were shown to a wooden barrack room where we would spend the night. The corporal instructed everyone to leave the blankets, [three on each bed], folded neat and tidy next morning, because "many of you will not be returning to this particular billet after tomorrow." Asked why we were here, he replied that he didn't know, and could not discuss each individual case, but this was a Physical Development Centre [PDC], and that we would be starting on a nine-week course of training that would get increasingly more strenuous. What did he mean by "each individual case"? As he was about to leave he added, "Be outside at 05:25 ready to march off for dinner." We were.

The mess hall was the same yet different from Copthorne. Long tables, just the same. Propaganda notices, just the same. Line up for food, just the same, but the atmosphere was not the same. The food was better, and a notice proclaimed one could eat as much as one wanted, but if you took more and did not consume it, you would be placed on a "charge".

Naturally, that evening, the inhabitants of hut No. 8 tried to figure out what happened at this PDC place? One fellow, out of the South Wales Borderers, mentioned he was there because his back was not quite straight. Another because he had trouble with his feet. What was wrong with me I wondered? This was a real puzzle, which would only be resolved after a night's sleep, a sleep interrupted several times by wailing air raid sirens, thunderous anti-aircraft fire, and distant exploding bombs.

The next morning after breakfast, these assorted "soldiers" marched off to one of four large gymnasiums. One by one our names were called and we presented ourselves at the designated table, behind which sat two medical officers and a note taking corporal. After many questions and a brief examination, one of the doctors explained why I was there. In addition to being underweight for my height and age, there was a lack of muscle in some parts of my torso.

So the mystery was resolved at last. The interview ended with instructions to join a particular group designated "B" platoon. Our sergeant for the next nine weeks would be a physical training instructor, and not the usual barrack square disciplinary type NCO. However, do not be misled. These sub-standard warriors were not to be deprived of the pleasures of "square bashing", but nothing like the Copthorne barrack performances.

Our future mentor, a tall, slender, slightly balding fellow approached and introduced himself as Sergeant Vincent Bloor. Then, after a few words about the barracks, he proceeded to describe the intensive training program we would be following over the next nine weeks. Everywhere in the army it seemed the training was always described as intensive.

There would be 40 minutes physical training under various names, followed by a return to the billet to change into battle dress or denim fatigue gear. 10 minutes would be allowed to accomplish this and parade outside again. After 40 minutes of drill, fatigues, or assault course, we would be given 10 minutes to change back into PT gear and be outside the billet again. This, he informed us, would be the routine for our stay here, with a few exceptions. Some would be given special exercises in an endeavor to rectify their particular problem, and the reason why they had been sent here. These special exercises would be performed whenever we reported to the gym, but especially on the 40 minutes shown on the notice board program as "remedial exercises". The inmates of this PDC were not only ordinary privates and NCOs. A captain who turned out to be the son of an Earl was also in our "platoon", although obviously, he didn't share our billet or our food and was always requested to "fall out" before we common privates were given that order.

A few weeks later, I found out that this soft-spoken, popular Sergeant Bloor was no other than the pre-war goalkeeper of the famous Aston Villa Football [soccer] Club. He was always there offering assistance and encouragement to those fellows experiencing difficulty performing any of the remedial exercises. He was also helpful in many other ways.

I recall breaking my bayonet in an attempt to repair the springs on my bed. Damaging the king's equipment is a chargeable offense. [Had I known it was George VI's bayonet, he could have had it back with pleasure]. When I informed Sergeant Bloor, he took me to the company office, filled out a form stating there was a flaw in the bayonet, and that it had been broken whilst tackling the battle course. This enabled me to obtain a replacement from the QM's store. What a relief, for I was certain I was going to be placed on a "charge".

Another recruit, Alf Welin, had great difficulty crossing over the catwalk and jumping the stream on the assault course. Sergeant Bloor would encourage and help him negotiate the catwalk with the aid of a long stick. Alf managed to do it towards the end of the nine weeks, but one could see the strain on his face. The sergeant also tried, but never succeeded, to get Alf to jump the stream. Poor chap, he was so embarrassed he would try to conquer this predicament by practicing in his spare time. One could see the determination on his face as he charged at the stream, and then at the last second run through it, getting soaking wet. Why he could not complete this simple act has always remained a mystery to me.

Private Welin was a very reserved young man from Carshalton in Surrey who loved music, and over the short time we were together he and I became very good friends. Because we had this common interest in music, conversations on the subject were many. Not only did he teach me a great deal about the subject, but we also attended several concerts and recitals together. He even managed to get me to see an opera, *Madame Butterfly*.

The entire platoon was pleased when eventually Alf was posted to a non-combative unit at York. It was here, whilst on night duty, that an ATS officer discovered him practicing on the piano in her office. She was furious. What was he doing in her office, and what was he doing playing her precious piano? She was going to place him on a charge. However, after a few minutes of conversation the captain realized how knowledgeable and enthusiastic he was about music, and the few minutes became two hours. From then on, she allowed him to practice whenever he wished, as long as she was not on duty. Sometimes, Alf informed me, they would sit for hours, simply discussing the merits of a particular composer's works.

After the war, this same lady officer applied for Alf to take a rehabilitation course on music, a course only open to professional musicians whose studies had been interrupted by the conflict. He was turned down, but the officer appealed the decision and won. The board stated that although he was not a proficient player of an instrument, they would allow him to take the course due to his dedication to the subject and to the very exceptional circumstances. A nice little story, don't you think?

The temporary wooden billets in which we were housed had one huge drawback. There was nowhere one could get a bath. There were five or six showers in one of the other permanent buildings, but these had to be shared between two to three hundred men. Therefore, once a week, Thursday I believe, our platoon would march down to Kingston swimming pool for a shower and swim. Thank goodness, there was the Salvation Army, YMCA, and other canteens.

Two billets were joined together by a cross building that from above resembled a letter "H". Six washbasins and toilets were housed in this cross section, and one can only imagine the chaos that ensued when twenty to

Private Alf Welin

thirty men were trying to get a wash and shave in time for the first parade of the day. The mess that duty privates had to clean up was beyond words.

The first two weeks at Kingston were like hell on earth. Aches and pains appeared in all parts of the body. All day long, it was PT, square bashing [drill], PT, fatigues, PT, battle course, and PT. There was even PT after PT. How could one endure this for nine weeks? Answer: painstakingly, with the emphasis on the pain.

Drill on the parade ground was performed under the watchful eye of Sergeant Ames. Sergeant Bloor informed us that Ames had seen much action in North Africa and had been decorated for his bravery. Terribly wounded, he had been invalided home and assigned his present job.

Sergeant Ames heralded from the east end of London, and possessed a strong Cockney accent and manner. If I close my eyes, I can see him still. He was a formidable character, always impeccably turned out, easily recognized by his stance and by the stylish way in which he marched. The recruits would fall in, and he would slowly walk up and down in front of his troops, describing what he intended to teach that session. He had a wonderful staccato way of speaking, and would always start off by saying, ")n the parade graurnd... all sorts of... wonderful... and weird movements... can be executed... and to-dye... we will be... learning... how to... sulow march," all the time tossing his head in time with every few words. Another thing about this awesome instructor was his facial expressions. He would stretch his face muscles, bare his teeth [they reminded me of a piano keyboard, minus the black notes], and as he ranted on, spittle would fly in all directions. The front rank was definitely not the place to be.

Richmond Park is situated about half a mile from Kingston on Thames barracks, and it was here that most of our route marches and runs [in both PT gear and battle order] took place. It is a park renowned for its large royal home, White Lodge, its herds of deer, and pleasant wooded areas. It was here that King George VI and Queen Elizabeth made their first home. At that time, it also housed rows and rows of searchlights and 3.7 Anti-aircraft guns. Is it any wonder the inhabitants around there, including we barrack inmates, found it hard to get to sleep at night?

A six-mile route march through and around Richmond Park was scheduled for the third Friday of the course, and what a revelation this turned out to be, at least it was for me.

Moss, from the Green Howards, had a sort of "wavy navy" way of marching. His foot would go forward, and then his body would move in a sort of "S" motion until the head lined up with his feet again. He was most difficult to march behind, so poor old Moss was always relegated to the last row.

However, the biggest surprise was a personal one. After about four miles, a big tough looking fellow named Cohen could not keep up, and it looked as though he would drop by the wayside. Sergeant Bloor had a few words with him, but Cohen was determined to finish. The sergeant then relieved him of his rifle and handed it to me, and that's how I finished the march, carrying two rifles. A lorry came around at intervals to pick up anyone who was deemed to be in a bad way. Nevertheless, some chaps' feet were bleeding at the end of it all and had to receive medical treatment.

Learning from all this, I henceforth followed an exercise imparted to me by my Scout Master, Bill Chesworth. The night before a route march, my socks would be turned inside out, a generous amount of soap applied to the soles, toe and heel areas and allowed to dry overnight. What a difference this made. Next morning, before putting them on my feet, the socks were turned the right side out. As the feet got hot, the soap acted like a lubricant. The result — no blisters.

My remedial exercises consisted of "shins to the beam" and "V sits" only. Others attended for "contrast foot baths". This entailed dipping one's feet in hot water for a couple of minutes, then placing them in some very cold liquid. A few fellows had loops attached to their toes, which in turn where attached to weights over a pulley. This wiggling of toes was called — you've guessed it — "weights and pulleys". I could never understand what this exercise was supposed to accomplish.

Ah, but a great discovery was made during that first week. Wonder of wonders, there was an ex-tailor on the staff, and he did alterations to uniforms in his spare time. He, with the aid of his sewing machine, was making a fortune. For the princely sum of five shillings, both my battledresses were finally modified to fit my manly frame. At last I could walk abroad and not feel as though people were staring and laughing at me.

Thus, on the 2nd weekend at Kingston, smartly turned out, Dave and I ventured up to the big city. The train took us up to Waterloo, and from there we made our way to the Tottenham Court Road YMCA, which we had heard was very good. After a lovely bath, and a nice meal [nine pence], yet another terrific discovery was made. Major Glen Miller and the band of the USA Expeditionary Force played at the Queensbury Club every Thursday night. "Who's Glen Miller?" asked Dave. I couldn't believe it. How could anyone not have heard of the great Glen Miller?

Directions on how to get to this club were obtained, and I hauled Dave over there. By this time, it was about 5:30 PM, and a queue had already formed outside, which we joined. Famous and not so famous movie and stage artists had taken over the enormous London Casino Theatre and presented shows every night of the week. The cost to enroll in the club was one shilling for six months. What a bargain!

That evening, as we entered, who should be handing out programs but Teddy Wilson [a famous and very popular music hall artist], and a film actress whose name escapes me. The same goes for most of the bill that night, although I do recall soldiers, sailors, and airmen of all nationalities striding onto that huge stage and dancing to Henry Hall and the BBC Dance Orchestra.

So every Thursday evening after "fall out", Dave and I would hurriedly smarten ourselves up and race to join the line up outside the Queensbury Club. This Glen Miller Orchestra, of course, was very different from his civilian orchestra, numbering about 50 strong, with a large string section. Such memorable names such as Jerry Gray, Tex Beneke, and the Crew Chiefs come to mind. The Thursday night show was always broadcast at 8:00 PM, but the orchestra would play for half an hour before and after. A few minutes before 8:00, the orchestra would stop playing and start re-tuning their instruments. Then right on the top of the hour the orchestra would strike up with "Moonlight Serenade", the announcer would point to the side of the stage and declare, "Ladies and gentlemen — Major Glen Miller," and the theatre would erupt with applause. How can one forget wonderful tunes like "American Patrol", "Jukebox Saturday Night", "In the Mood" and "Little Brown Jug"?

One night Glen Miller announced the next piece would be "String of Pearls", and the arranger, Sergeant Jerry Gray, would conduct it. A spotlight flashed to the top of one of the sweeping stairs that led from the first balcony onto the stage, and Jerry strolled down to take the baton. I have never forgotten that night, and of course, the tune became yet another great Glen Miller classic.

Months later, the music world would be stunned, when the plane taking Glen Miller to France, went missing over the English Channel. It became one of the great mysteries of the war, when neither the plane nor any of its occupants were ever found.

Many of the artists appearing at the Queensbury Club, were already big stars. Harry Roy, Jack Payne, Tommy Handley, Flanagan and Allen, Zoe Gail, [a wonderful dancer who, shortly after I saw her, lost both her legs in an air raid], Max Miller, Anne Shelton, Jack Buchanan, Elsie and Doris Waters,

Frankie Howard, Billy Bennet, the Western Brothers, and of course Vera Lynn. One evening a young schoolgirl was introduced, and out from the wings walked Petula Clark. She would become a big star after the war. How I wished I had kept those programs.

The happy times spent at that club were one side of the war. There was, unfortunately, also the gruesome side. One such event happened on a Saturday at around 1:00 PM. A pub near the entrance to Waterloo Station had received a direct hit during the previous night's bombing, and rescue work was still going on at the time we walked out of the station. We scrambled our way past the pub's skeletal remains and the 12 to 15 bodies lying in a row on the roadway waiting to be removed. Unbelievably, David and I strode by with hardly a glance. It was a few hours later when I suddenly recalled the tragic scene we had witnessed. Had we actually walked by all those corpses, with not second glance, as if it was an everyday occurrence, which, in fact, is exactly what it was? Had I become so hard that the sight of death meant nothing to me? Did I not care about those poor people? How strange it seemed that two young teenagers, who, until recently, had led reasonably tranquil lives, could so quickly get used to all this horror and destruction.

Privates [Unknown], Welin, Eadie, and Gilbert

Private Bert Eadie, a native of Fulham, had been an apprentice engraver before being drafted into the army. What he hoped to do after the war, was design and produce the fancy Gothic scroll work one sees in Bibles and other religious books. Another of his ambitions was to design stamps and coins. One morning he was called to the company office and given 48 hours compassionate leave. During the previous night's bombing his family's home had received a direct hit, and the police had phoned to ask if the army could spare him for a couple of days. As Fulham is only about an hour away, the CO had agreed. Luckily, his parents and sister had been in a nearby air raid shelter, but were in a terrible state of shock, as they had lost everything.

Bert related this sad tale upon his return. He said he just couldn't believe it. He turned the corner into his street, and about a dozen houses were nothing more than a mass of rubble. Of their lovely semi-detached home, nothing was left.

One could not, officially, take animals or pets into the air raid shelters, so Mr. Eadie had placed Bert's dog down in the cellar with lots of water, food and his blanket. Bert, fighting back the tears, then described how his father told him his pet had somehow escaped from the ruins and gone berserk. After a while the police cornered and shot the poor thing. There was nothing else they could do.

Another weekend we decided to visit St. Paul's cathedral, the great Christopher Wren masterpiece. The sight that greeted our eyes can only be described as both spectacular and amazing. Amazing, because for about one hundred yards around this massive place of worship, practically every building had been demolished, giving an uninterrupted view of the famous landmark. How could German bombs have fallen all around and yet miss this huge target? Perhaps St. Paul himself had taken a hand in protecting his church.

St. Paul's, of course, did receive a few direct hits, mostly from incendiaries, but thanks to the small army of volunteer fire watchers who patrolled the cathedral by day and night, damage was kept to a minimum. These brave people even had a group patrolling high in the great dome at the height of the bombing. What is more, the only equipment these ordinary, [some people would say they were extraordinary], men and women had to fight the firebombs with were buckets of water complete with stirrup pump, and sandbags. Incendiary bombs were small, [about a foot long by 2 or 3 inches diameter], and came down in showers, but if one acted promptly, they could be smothered with a sand bag before the flames could get a foothold.

On yet another Sunday afternoon, Alf Welin and I paid another visit St. Paul's to see and listen to the great Dame Myra Hess give a free piano recital. Wonderful!

It became increasingly evident to me that even in those few weeks away from home my whole horizon had been vastly expanded by the variety of people I had met and by the sights and sounds I had experienced. It was as if a completely new world had opened up.

The weeks rolled by and soon it was Christmas. Parades were canceled for that special day and for boxing day, but no leave passes were granted. Some of the fellows thought there might be a lull in the air raids for the festive season, but alas, this was not to be. Christmas Eve was particularly bad. A few decorations appeared in the dining hall, and everyone who wanted could attend their individual church services, but it was not what one would call a "Merry Christmas".

On Christmas Day, the whole barracks assembled in the dining room for dinner, and true to army tradition, the lower officers and NCOs waited upon the ordinary ranks. A plump middle-aged lady performed on the piano, and the place rang out with a few carols and songs like "Roll Out the Barrel" and 'There'll Always Be an England". However, it was not like being at home with one's family. Unfortunately, some fellows had to be on guard duty, and so missed some of the fun, but alas, war does not stop for Christmas.

Strange as it may seem, I actually began to enjoy all the hard training. My weight increased, and muscles appeared all over the place. Even my muscles had muscles. I don't think I have ever been so fit in all my life, and I could have willingly stayed there for the rest of the war, but alas, King George VI had other plans for Private Gilbert 524.

Every three weeks a medical examination took place, and where necessary, revisions made to the remedial exercises and/or special treatments. Some of the results were amazing, whilst others were not so good. A case in point was Private Moss, who still marched in his terrible "wavy navy" way at the termination of the course.

Towards the end of the nine weeks, on Saturday morning, everyone had to pass a final rigorous test carried out in full battle order, before being sent on to complete their interrupted primary training. This test consisted of carrying a soldier of comparable height and weight to oneself for one hundred yards. You in your turn were carried back by your buddy to the start line. Then it was off on a one and a half mile run and walk [minus one's rifle], through Richmond Park, finishing back in the barrack square. Five minutes were allowed to rest and collect the remainder of your section, and then it was off on a ten-mile route march. All this to be accomplished within three and a half hours. The day before, everyone in the billet was saying it could not be done, but we did it, confounding even ourselves. If we passed, the reward was a thirty-six hours pass, which meant I could go home for the first time in eleven weeks. That was the biggest incentive of all to beat the clock.

Shortly after twelve o'clock, all my successful section raced through the barrack gates, along Richmond Road, down the High Street, and into the railway station. At Waterloo Station, it was down the tube and over to Euston Station, where the LMS train would take me home to Stafford. As usual, the train was packed with soldiers, sailors, airmen, WAAFs, ATS, and WRENS of all nationalities. There were, at this point in history, servicemen and women from all the occupied countries of Europe, and from all over the British Empire and Commonwealth, plus the Americans. It was an amazing time. It was an exciting time.

Example: stationed in my small hometown itself, and in the surrounding countryside and villages, were contingents of Canadians, British, Free French, Poles, Czechs, Norwegians, and black and white Americans. All got on reasonably well together, except for the Americans.

A nearly completed new technical college in the centre of town had been taken over by the British army in 1939, but was vacated in 1942, and assigned to black American troops. Out to the south of town in the grounds of Shugborough Hall, [the ancestral home of the Earls of Lichfield], a large base and hospital was manned by American white troops. Many of the white US troops did not like black troops dancing and talking to white English girls, so on many Saturday nights fights would break out in the dance halls, pubs, and streets. This sort of behavior was completely foreign to the English, who just couldn't understand it. After all, were we not all fighting for the same cause? The right of all people to live free from discrimination and oppression? On those nights, military policemen, [mostly American, who were referred to as "Snowdrops", because of their white helmets], were out in force. They stood no nonsense. They would wade in with their "billy clubs" hammering anyone who got in their way. It was not a pleasant sight.

One day, 50 odd years later, I asked Stafford Bidwell, a fellow member of The Ancient Mariners, a senior's canoe club in Cambridge, Ontario, Canada, how he came by his first name?

"There has always been a Stafford in my family," he replied. Then before he could say another word, his wife Audrey, interrupted with, "And do you know Vinnie, he was stationed at this little town called Stafford in England during the war."

As you can imagine, we talked for quite some time about my birthplace, and discovered we both used to go to the same dance hall and local pub — namely, the Borough Hall, and the Rose and Crown. Who knows, perhaps we had even been there on the same nights. It's a small world.

Those few hours at home, when mother had her baby boy to fuss over again for a short time, passed by in a flash. Everyone commented on how fit and well I looked, and wanted to know about the barracks, the training, the food, my companions, and the bombing.

During the war, when everything was rationed, food ration stamps would be issued to any serviceman who was lucky enough to be granted one, two, or three weeks leave, but this was not the case for a 36-hour pass. How people survived on these meager portions, I will never understand, but they did. What's more, the standard of health went up. All bread was whole wheat, no white bread at all.

The following will give the reader an idea of how stringent these weekly rations per person were: bacon — 2ozs, sugar — 4ozs., butter — 2ozs., eggs — 1, milk — 3 pints, meat — 1 shilling and 6 pence worth, and petrol only in very special cases [*i.e.* for a doctor]. Sixty clothing coupons had to last for a year, and if one was getting married, the couple received coupons to purchase a few pieces of utility furniture. As the reader can imagine, my feeling of guilt was great when my mother presented me with two whole rashers of bacon, one egg and fried bread for breakfast on Sunday morning.

After 3 months in the army, my twenty and a half hours at home came quickly to an end, and 2:30 PM Sunday found me back at the railway station awaiting the train for the return journey to Kingston on Thames. As usual, the train was packed to the seams. I could have left by a later train, but it meant the risk of being caught in an air raid, and also it was not much fun trying to get around London in the blacked out streets.

Monday morning came and it was announced that many of us "graduates" would be traveling north to Bradford in Yorkshire to complete our basic training. Many were sorry to be leaving Kingston on Thames, but you have to go where the army sends you. Erroneously, we thought it was just another posting, little realizing it would turn out to be a nightmare of a place.

Chapter Three
Bradford

How can one describe Manningham Lane Barracks? It was not exactly hell, but it was perhaps a purgatory, and it was on a bleak, cold, late January afternoon that we arrived at these [so-called] barracks. Grey dirty snow fell from an even greyer and dirtier sky. It was a lovely day for a funeral. In fact, nearly every day spent at this establishment was a lovely day for a funeral.

On leaving the station, the new arrivals were met by several MPs who, after inspecting each soldier's posting documents, instructed our group to throw our kitbags into lorry no. 2 and form up over there, which we did. When all had assembled, we were brought to "attention", "right turned", and upon the order, marched briskly towards the unknown.

Bradford was definitely not a pretty city. I say, "was", because I sincerely hope things have changed over the years. At that time, there was row upon row of miserable looking terraced houses, interspersed with menacing looking factories belching out soot-laden smoke. Perhaps I'm being a little too harsh, but I thought it an ugly, hilly, neglected place. Who knows, maybe coping with these abject surroundings is what made the men and woman of this northern city so friendly, cheerful, and generous to a fault.

Marching through the barrack gates, we turned right and came to a halt in the "barrack square". This 'square', [rectangle really], had a slope of about 5 degrees and was surrounded on three sides by a high wall crowned with barbed wire and concrete embedded broken glass. At the bottom of this gradient was a row of shed-like buildings that had been given the grandiose title of "dining room" by some faceless dreamer who was obviously in dire need of psychiatric treatment.

To our front lay a long, ugly, sombre, morbid building, the entrance to which could only be approached by marching up a thirty-degree ramp. The order was given to march up this ramp in single file, pass through the side door, turn left and left again, into what was supposed to be the NAAFI canteen.

Once inside, we were in fact directed left and left again, by two stern, depressed looking corporals. All this happened so quickly it was virtually impossible to get a good look at our new home. However, from what I glimpsed, I was not impressed. Why didn't they let everyone get rid of all their gear before taking them into the NAAFI, I wondered? Private Gilbert 524 was soon to find out!

In the canteen, tables had been pushed to one side, and after being ordered to rid ourselves of our backpacks, we took our seats on the rows of chairs in front of a small raised dais. At the rear of this, fixed to the wall, was a layout of the "barracks" showing, what appeared to be rows and rows of oblong boxes. Immediately everyone was settled down, the sergeant major mounted the platform and introduced himself and our new sergeant — Henson. He informed us we would be here for six weeks primary intensive training, [which we already knew], and then proceeded to break several pieces of "good" news.

He told us that this was the second time that day he had given this lecture, so remember you are not alone. What sort of a place had we arrived at to be given a welcoming speech that started with, "remember, you are not alone"? He pointed to a section of boxes on the diagram and stated that these represented the double bunk beds and small space we would be occupying for the duration of the time spent here. Locks for all kitbags must be purchased, [no lockers here], and every piece of equipment must be marked, especially boots.

After a few more words, he handed over to Captain Cartwright, who then gave out more "good" news. "Before the war", he began, "this had been the local territorial, [reserve part time], army drill hall, and so to accommodate new recruits the hall has been fitted out with hundreds of bunk beds. I realize it is most unsuitable, but in times of war, we all have to make sacrifices." I liked the "we". Then came the final bombshell!

"You" he said, "together with about one hundred other trainees, are the only ones here who have not got a criminal record. Roughly 30% of your fellow trainees have been transferred here directly from either a military or civilian prison." We never did find out why and how this had come about, no matter how much some people tried.

Captain Cartwright continued, "These people have records for theft, robbery with violence, fraud, rape, and one for murder, a charge reduced to manslaughter for lack of evidence. For this reason, lights will be left on 24 hours a day, and there will be special guard duties."

"One is called 'roving guard', when four armed soldiers wearing plimsolls, [running shoes], will be walking up and down the rows of bunks all night. The other is 'balcony guard'. This will consist of two soldiers who will be stationed on the small balcony at the end of the hall. These guards will have the rows of bunks under scrutiny at all times. I must warn you all, that should you discover any part of your equipment is missing, we are required by King's Regulations to place you on a charge. This we realize is most unfair, but that's the way it has to be. Boots are the most prized item these people steal, because they can be easily sold on the black market. The staff sympathizes with you, but we also have to follow orders. Just be careful whom you talk to, what you say, and do not be misled. One last thing, all soldiers performing these guard duties will be chosen from you people and from other units in the area. None of the criminal element will be called upon to perform these duties. This again may appear unfair, but experience has shown that this is the only way to ensure top security."

What an introduction! Horrible billets, horrible fellow inmates, and soon we were to find out, horrible food. The place was a nightmare. Even with the lights on and the patrolling guards, kitbags were cut open and boots stolen. Not mine, thank goodness. How the thieves managed to hide their loot and to get their ill-gotten gains past the guards on the gate, [always from other nearby units, and never from inside our own establishment], we could never fathom out.

Even after all these years, if I close my eyes, I can still picture the place, vivid and exact. An episode in my life best forgotten, but alas forever remembered.

Ahead was the longest six weeks of my life. I'm sure there will be some readers who will smile and say to themselves, "Poor old Vinnie has got to be exaggerating just a little bit." Please believe me, I most certainly am not. If only the reader could have experienced the place, smelled the smells, tasted the food, endured the horrible atmosphere, and gone through the routine of checking all his equipment and personal gear whenever he returned to his bunk. If only he or she could listen to the noises throughout the night, half asleep, half awake, all the time making sure one's few possessions were safely tucked away. If you could have experienced those appalling conditions, then all your doubts would be dispelled immediately.

Obviously, avoiding the criminal types became one of our main objectives, but in such a confining situation it was virtually impossible. Some were quite nice looking fellows, and one would never have guessed they were confidence tricksters, robbers, or rapists. Others had that gangster-like attitude and appearance. However, standing out from this crowd, was one particular inmate whose nasty, sallow face I can only describe as cadaverous and who gave everyone the shivers. He looked like two pence worth of death warmed up.

Bert Eadie was quite a proficient artist, and he produced some excellent black and white sketches of the 'barracks' with a few added touches, like a machine gun mounted on the balcony, and whip-armed Nazi storm troopers marching up and down the rows of bunks. How I wish I had one of those sketches now. I wonder if he kept any of them?

The great compensation in this sad looking Yorkshire city was the people of Bradford, who were absolutely wonderful. No other description fits the bill. It was as if they knew of the dreadful conditions we were being made to endure and were expressing their sympathy. The instances of kindness were so many, and the services provided at the many volunteer canteens so good, I feel I must relate a few.

Nearby, there was a fish and chip shop, that Bert, Alf, Dave, and I would call into occasionally and place our order. The person behind the counter would hand over the little package, I would give her the money, then sometimes she would say something like, "Just a minute lad, don't forget your change," and hand me back my money or more change than was required. At the canteens, especially the one in Forster Square, the meals were good and cheap. One could also get a nice bath, and women would ask if you wanted any socks darned or repairs to clothing. Many were the times when a serviceman was invited to one of the volunteer's homes to share their meager rations for Sunday dinner.

There was a story about a soldier who asked one lady volunteer to sit at his table and just nag him. "Why do you want me to do that?" she asked.

"Because I miss my wife, and I'm feeling terribly homesick", came the reply.

On the buses, the ticket collector would shuffle along the aisle calling out, "Any more fares? Any more fares?" Servicemen and women would hold up their pennies, but he or she would just pass them by as if they didn't exist. Not once did I pay a bus fare.

Alf Welin continued to amaze me with his knowledge of music. "Why," I asked, "haven't you made music your career, or learned to play an instrument?" His reply was, "I never had the opportunity, and my parents certainly couldn't afford to send me to a music school or teacher." I knew this must be true, because my parents had been in the same situation. It was in Bradford that Alf persuaded me to attend a local theatre to see a touring production of *Madame Butterfly*. Although I now realize it must have been a second rate production, at the time I thought it was wonderful.

One should also remember, 1943/44 was one of the worst winters on record, and this, coupled with our awful accommodation, did not improve things. If only the sun had shone for a few days it might have helped, but all the time we were there, it was cold, cloudy, damp, and every few days a little more snow would fall.

There must have been three to four hundred men billeted in that drill hall, and yet there were only about ten toilets and washbasins, no shower facilities and no baths. It was disgusting and depressing. It was all so "Heath Robinson". Alf and I figured that if we lined up around 8:00 o'clock in the evening, we could get a wash and shave, and that would last us until the next evening. We would also take a mug of cold water back to our bunk. In the morning, we would splash this onto our face, and that would be our ablutions for the day.

It was with dread that I used the toilets, and the advice given by my brother Horace and his wife, before leaving home for Copthorne Barracks in Shrewsbury, came flooding back. On one such visit, some bright inmate had written on the wall, "It's no use standing on the seat, the crabs in here can jump six feet." My trips to this essential place were as a last resort.

Naturally, we discussed the situation among ourselves, and decided the harsh reality was that we just had to make the best of it. After all, we thought, six weeks isn't too long — but it was long enough. Some were all for writing to their Members of Parliament. Whether anyone did or not I can't recall.

During those few weeks, a couple of fellows who wilted under the conditions went AWOL, [absent without leave], but they were soon arrested, returned to Manningham Lane, and charged. They were picked up at their homes. Both were confined to Chorley Military Prison for a month, and of course, they were returned to Manningham Lane to complete their primary training.

The "dining room" was furnished with square tables and benches, and it would only hold a limited number of people. After the diners were seated, two men from each table were designated to proceed to a counter and bring back round tins full of "food". One day, we discovered several one inch diameter by five inches long 'off-white tinged with brown' things in the tin. Courageously, one of the fellows prodded these mysterious objects with a fork several times, to find out if they were still alive, and after much discussion, it was decided that these "things" were actually sausages. They were un-sausages. Bert suggested these could be one of Hitler's secret weapons. Now, whenever I see a sausage I automatically think of Manningham Lane. The food was like pigswill, but what could one do? One had to eat. No wonder moral was low. Complaints were made to the orderly officer, but nothing changed.

One mealtime the round tin placed on the table contained some black-brownish things that immediately brought the question from Private Eadie, "What are they?"

After much prodding with a fork, Private Sanders replied, "I think they're some sort of rissole."

"Rissole," stated Private Barker, "they look and taste, [nibble, nibble], more like Jack Johnson's arse hole". Johnson was a black American heavy weight boxing champion. Somebody else sarcastically added, "Please give my compliments to the chef would you."

The "Gymnasium" was situated in a nearby dilapidated building that in its time had been a church, then a club, and last of all a dance hall. The condition of the "Ideal Ballroom" complimented the barracks. Puddles of water were everywhere due to the leaky roof, and there was no heating at all. The platoon would be marched down wearing army greatcoats over their PT kit. It was like stepping out onto the Siberian tundra, but then, once there, the greatcoats had to be removed in order to perform the physical exercises. It really is amazing that no one died of pneumonia or exposure.

Bayonet practice was one of the things I absolutely loathed. It was beyond my imagination, how anyone could ram a bayonet into a fellow human being, even if he was the enemy. It worried me, and I wondered if I would be able to do it. "Of course you will," the instructor remarked. "If the time comes when it's you or him, you will do it." They were probably right, but it still weighed heavily upon my mind.

This practice training took place in Manningham Lane Stadium, the home of Bradford City Football Club. About twenty years after the war, part of this same stadium caught fire during a regular Saturday afternoon football league game. It was completely destroyed with the loss of many lives.

The ground was not exactly on Manningham Lane, but about a hundred yards or so down a side street. Upon arrival, the platoon would line up across the end of the football field, and the order given to "fix bayonets". While Sergeant Henson gave instructions, a corporal, with the aid of a dummy, would demonstrate how to attack the enemy. Afterwards, the platoon would advance in line abreast towards the opposite end of the football pitch, all the time endeavoring to keep the tip of the bayonet as still as possible. The sergeant and corporals would, for a time, walk backwards, making sure the line was kept straight and the rifles held in the correct position. If a wavering bayonet was spotted, the whole wrath of the sergeant would be directed towards the unlucky private.

Upon reaching the far end, half would turn to the left and the other half to the right, then sprint around the perimeter back to the initial starting point. This was repeated several times, after which, wooden frames holding straw dummies would be positioned near the far end of the field. This time as we advanced, the order was given to "double march", [a sort of slow run]. At the order "charge", everyone started to run faster, screaming and shouting, and upon reaching the dummies, the bayonet was forced home into the "enemy". The next action was to stick ones boot against the impaled "body", twist the bayonet, withdraw it and then strike your opponent in the face with the butt of the rifle. All very charming.

Towards the end of our stay, many days were spent on Ilkley Moor. Army lorries would provide the transport, and in full battle order, we would be shuttled off to this desolate, bleak, frost encrusted Yorkshire landscape. There was always a biting wind blowing across the moor, making it feel colder than it really was. Looking into the distance, one could imagine the stark grey house known as Wuthering Heights being just over the horizon. I almost expected Heathcliff to make a guest appearance.

After our first visit to the moor, I made sure to wear double underwear and double anything else that wouldn't restrict movement too much.

Here, recruits were instructed on the correct way to lie on the ground in order to fire the rifle. NCOs walked along the line, moving this leg or that arm, and sometimes the whole body into the acceptable position. This went on for half an hour or so. While we were lying on the ground, freezing to death, the NCOs were ensconced in their greatcoats, scarfs, balaclavas [and no doubt, double underwear], walking up and down flapping their arms to keep warm.

After loosing off one magazine [5 bullets] from our Lee-Enfields, it was time to tackle the assault course. With bayonets fixed, we would crawl under barbed wire, through tunnels, swing on ropes, climb walls, cross catwalks, all the time being goaded on by the instructors.

At lunchtime there was a break for sandwiches, US Army K-rations, [tinned concentrated food], and soup. I never did find out where this food came from, but it was far better than the garbage served out at Manningham

Lane.

This was followed by grenade throwing exercises, and on our last trip to the moor, we were given the great pleasure of throwing live hand grenades. Six at a time, we were taken out to a distant five-foot deep trench. The idea was to pull the pin from the grip and throw the grenade with a cricket bowling action towards a steel pole about 50 yards away. The thrower would then duck down into the trench, and by the time one had counted up to ten, the grenade would explode. On the way back to Manningham Lane we heard that one fellow had only thrown the grenade about ten yards, [someone said his feet had slipped on the mud], and just stood there looking at it. Luckily, the instructor saw what happened, took a dive at the thrower, both of them landing in the bottom of the trench just as the thing exploded. You can bet your life the instructor had a nice little chat with the errant thrower, with a few blasphemies for good measure

For a finale, and to finish off these most enjoyable days, we young warriors would crawl through the assault course once again, holding our rifles between our arms, while live ammunition whistled overhead, at a height of 3 or 4 feet. This took about half an hour. It seemed like three. One stayed on the ground until ordered to stand and return to the starting point. Happy campers we were not. Around 16:00 hours, these frozen, mud caked, fed up soldiers re-embarked onto the lorries to be driven back to the barracks.

Oh, the joy of it all. I hadn't had so much fun since having my appendix removed.

And so the weeks slowly passed, until on the last Friday of our stay, a day all had been looking forward to with great anticipation, the postings went up on the notice board. Alf would join a Royal Army Ordnance Corps unit at York. Dave would report to the Royal Warwickshire Regiment. Bert would become a member of the Royal Tank Corps. And Gilbert would join the ranks of the 22nd Anti-tank Regiment, Royal Artillery, stationed at Shoeburyness in Essex. It was sad to be parted from new friends, but the joy on leaving Manningham Lane could not be hidden. However, I was not the only one who contemplated what our new posting would be like, and if the local population of these new locations would be as kind and generous as the people of Bradford.

Tuesday morning arrived, and we said farewell to one another, promising to keep in touch, but very few did. Alf Welin and I corresponded for many years, even after the war, but gradually the interval between letters became longer and longer, until this also ceased. How I regret it now.

I did have the good fortune to reconnect with one of those soldiers in

2005. My old friend Alice Wilberforce and her daughter had rented a holiday cottage on a farm just outside Ludlow in England. One day, while chatting to the farmer, he happened to mention that he was on his way to visit his old neighbor at Ashford Court Farm who had recently suffered a stroke. Strange as it may seem, Alice recalled me telling her about an old army buddy who lived at a place called Ashford Court Farm, and after relating my story to her landlord asked if she could accompany him.

After being introduced to the old man, she asked if he had been in the army during the war, and if he had been stationed at Kingston on Thames. "Yes", he replied, and after a few more questions it came about that he was indeed my old friend David Webb. Alice took down his phone number, and upon her return home to Oakville, Ontario, Canada, I phoned him. It really is a small world.

On the morning of departure, kitbags were loaded onto waiting lorries, the troops formed up, and to the sound of great cheers, and a few disparaging remarks, these bold fighting men marched out of the same foreboding gates they had entered six weeks earlier.

Had it only been six weeks?

At the station, kitbags were thrown from the lorries into a great heap, and instantly, there was a mad rush to make sure yours did not fall into the hands of one of our criminal friends. This accomplished, the troops lined up in three ranks again. As names were called out, privates stepped forward, collected their travel documents, and proceeded to the designated platform. True to form, a few minutes before my train arrived, and before squeezing my way into one of the carriages, it started to snow. Quite appropriate really, for we had arrived in the snow, and we were departing in the snow.

I will never, [for very opposite reasons], forget Manningham Lane nor the people of Bradford!

Once again, I was traveling south. The carriages were damp with condensation, and every now and then a little rivulet would trickle down the window. No one spoke, and everyone appeared to be wrapped up in their own thoughts. I was interested in the passing countryside, so I wiped a small area with my glove, enough to see through. Gradually, with each passing mile, the scenery became softer and gentler. Town followed town, and county followed county, until eventually the train slowly puffed its way to a halt in Kings Cross Station, London. This time the RTO's instructions were for me to make my way across the bomb-scarred city to Fenchurch Street Railway station, and hence to Shoeburyness.

The next day, Private Gilbert 524, became Gunner Gilbert 524.

Chapter Four
Shoeburyness

Everyone, at some time in their lives, has had that certain feeling, call it intuition, when one senses a change is about to take place in one's life. It's hard to explain, but at the end of the journey as I walked out of Shoeburyness railway station, on that lovely early March sunny day, I just knew circumstances had changed for the better. Perhaps that's a ridiculous statement to make, because any place had to be better than Manningham Lane, but that huge orange circular thing in the sky shone down upon this young soldier for the first time since Kingston on Thames. It just had to be a good omen.

The two robust and expressionless military policemen, standing at the exit, didn't say a word, just pointed in the direction of the barracks. Luckily, the railway station was only a few hundred yards from the barrack gates. I say 'luckily', because these new arrivals were not only loaded down with the usual soldier's paraphernalia of rifle, greatcoat, backpacks, gas mask, steel helmet, *etc.*, but also had to shoulder their own kitbag.

The garrison town of Shoeburyness is located where the historic river Thames enters the North Sea. Looking south across the estuary, one could see Sheerness, and the Isle of Grain, while five miles to the west, the nearest large town, one that had cinemas, dance halls *etc.*, was Southend-on-Sea. Southend-on-mud would have been a more appropriate name, but looking at a map of the area, I suppose one could argue that Southend-on-Thames would be an even more correct label.

Like Copthorne in Shrewsbury, the construction of these barracks took place during Queen Victoria's reign, but that is where the comparison ended. Copthorne was built to accommodate an infantry regiment in a lovely,

43

ancient city, whereas Shoeburyness was designed solely as a Royal Artillery depot, and built at the last stop on the railway line, owned and operated by the London North Eastern Railway [LNER].

The greater part of the area adjacent to this garrison town, and for some miles along the coast, including the desolate and windswept firing range at Foulness, belonged to the Ministry of Defense, and most of the local inhabitants were directly or indirectly involved in the life of the garrison.

The garrison buildings were very much different from Copthorne, being well spaced out, and much more inviting. Whereas the KSLI barracks were of the long dormitory type construction, these billets were square in design. Over many decades, the facilities had been improved and the establishment expanded, so that it now covered several square miles. It even had its own small theatre and library.

After dragging myself into the guardroom, I handed over my posting documents and followed the now familiar procedure of applying a signature opposite my name on the presented list. Then, upon receiving further instructions, I stepped outside, struggled around the barrack square, and entered the designated new quarters.

It was a two story building with a spacious entrance hall, at the end of which lay the washrooms *etc.* Off this hallway were two rooms, and the one to the left, on the ground floor, was to be my new abode. My elation knew no bounds when I entered, for it was a large square room, complete with fireplace, accommodating just ten well-spaced out beds. At the foot of each bed was a wooden storage box, and over the head of the bed was an equally substantial wooden shelf. I discovered the following day that there were five gunners in a six-pounder anti-tank gun team, so obviously there were two teams to a room. There was another small room to the rear of the building, and this proved to be the Troop Bombardier's private quarters.

Everywhere was sparkling clean, including the ample toilets and showers, the latter of which I could not wait to take advantage. The large windows, criss-crossed with sticky tape [a safeguard against bomb blast and flying glass], looked out onto a tree-lined parade ground, and the trees were actually beginning to turn green. What a change from Bradford.

The layout of the upper floor was identical, which meant less time spent lining up for a wash, shower, or toilet. Twenty gunners upstairs and twenty gunners downstairs.

Before long, a slim, serious, but pleasant faced, medium height NCO with two stripes on his arms entered the room and requested our attention. All ten newcomers stood to attention. First, he stood the room "at ease", and then introduced himself.

"I am Troop Bombardier Poole," he informed us, "and you now belong to "C" Troop, 22nd Anti-tank Regiment, of the Royal Artillery. I ask, and expect your full co-operation during the three months of intensive training that lie ahead. It will not be a bed of roses, but with a little give and take I'm sure we will all get on well together." Then it was our turn to introduce ourselves and state where we came from and which primary training centre we had attended.

"Tomorrow," Troop Bombardier Poole continued, "you will meet the Troop Sergeant and Battery Sergeant Major. They are strict disciplinarians but extremely fair. You will also meet the Troop Commander, and the Battery Commander, Major McDowell. Each one of you should remember two things. One, if you do your best for them, they will reciprocate, and two, they know all the tricks, and can be twice as awkward with you as you can with them. You will also notice warning signs everywhere. You disregard these at your own peril. Okay?"

Coming to attention, we replied, "Yes Bombardier." Some, through force of habit replied, "Yes corporal," but quickly corrected themselves.

'C' Troop, 22nd Anti-tank Regiment, Royal Artillery

In the next few days, these new gunners found the aforementioned warning signs all over the place, many with skull and crossbones, especially along the pebble beach. Across these signs, in great bold letters, was emblazoned the cautionary words "Danger — minefield," "Restricted Area" and "Entrance

45

Prohibited". Only a small stretch of beach was accessible to the troops, the remainder being cordoned off with barbed wire entanglements. These signs were a reminder of that time [not so long ago], when Great Britain had stood alone for more than a year against the Axis powers, a time when the country, and indeed the whole world, anxiously awaited the expected German assault on these islands.

After describing the layout of the town and barracks, and pointing out where the quartermaster's store, sick bay, garrison theatre, NAAFI, dining room, church, and library was, he told the new occupants to proceed to the QM's store, where they would collect blankets, and a pillow. Then, just before leaving, he remarked, "Some of you have been unfortunate in your previous postings, but you will find this is a good, well organized depot. What you make of your stay here is up to you. Oh, and one last thing. Be outside at 17:25 hours ready to march off for dinner." When he mentioned "unfortunate postings", he looked directly at me, so I assumed he had encountered apprentice soldiers from Manningham Lane before. So ended this, my fourth, "welcome to the unit" speech.

Everyone was outside before 17:25 hours, for by then all these teenagers were ravenously hungry. The dining room was pleasant, with the usual posters about not wasting food, and careless talk costing lives. Best of all, the food was edible. I couldn't believe it! The sun was shining, the billets were palatial compared to Bradford, and the food was fit to eat. This was paradise.

Back at the barrack room, "black-out" curtains were put into place, beds were made, and the new inmates began to get acquainted. All this time, overhead, there had been the incessant drone of heavy bombers heading out towards the continent. The noise was such that we all sauntered outside to scan the sky, but couldn't see a thing. Whichever city was to be the target for that night, not one of our group had any sympathy for the Germans. Having witnessed what they had done to British and other European cities, we all agreed they were only getting their just desserts. On the other hand, it was sad to think that many of those planes would not return, and hundreds of gallant young men would lose their lives that night, or end up as prisoners of war.

Most of the new-comers were fast asleep in bed by 21:00 hours, including myself, but about half an hour later we were rudely awakened by wailing air raid sirens, and the whump, whump, whump of 3.7 anti-aircraft guns blazing away at German planes on their way to bomb poor old London. Hundreds of batteries had been sited all along the Thames estuary, and the noise was absolutely horrendous. Next morning we found that one 3.7 was only about 300 yards away from our billet. The strange thing was, as in the case of

Kingston, one soon got used to it and slept through it all.

It seems wherever one is posted in the army, that unit has a different way of doing things. Shoeburyness was no exception. The beds were steel, and the mattress comprised of "biscuits", three separate flat square sections to a bed. On the first morning there, Bombardier Poole demonstrated how beds were to be laid out for kit inspection each day, except Saturday and Sunday. The biscuits had to be laid on top of one another at the head of the bed. Blankets would be folded in the prescribed manner and arranged on top of the biscuits, while towels, boots and a few other bits and pieces, were displayed in a set manner on the spring portion of the bed, and, of course, all had to be in line. Only large and small packs, gas mask, steel helmet, and ammunition pouches were allowed on the shelf, in the prescribed order.

That little exercise over, we formed up outside, where we were eventually joined by our neighbours from upstairs, 'B' Troop. Strangely, there was no 'A' Troop. Be that as it may, as soon as it was ascertained everyone was present, the troops were brought to "attention" and marched on to the parade ground. Waiting for us there was Battery Sergeant Scott [I think that was his name] and the Regimental Sergeant Major, whose name I cannot recall. The troops [forty gunners], were brought to a halt, right turned, right faced, and given the order to stand at ease. Introductions were made and a description of our future training given.

"You are now proud members of the Royal Regiment of Artillery," the BSM announced, "and as such, you have a great tradition of service to uphold. Wherever action is taking place, there you will find the guns; hence, the motto of this regiment is 'ubique' — 'everywhere'. In addition, because we are 'everywhere', we are the only regiment in the British army that does not have its own colours. The guns are our colours; therefore you must always treat your guns with the greatest respect." As you will read later, some commanders took this "respect" to the most stupid and preposterous limits.

In due course, the troop and battery commanders arrived. With much foot slamming and pucka salutes, the BSM once again brought us to "attention" and reported to the major that "B and C troops present and correct sir." The major acknowledged the BSM with a more leisurely salute, and requested he stand the men at ease. Another smart "longest way up, shortest way down" salute, an about turn, and the order came, "Stand at — ease."

Each officer in turn extended a welcome to the 22nd Anti-tank Regiment, followed by a short patriotic speech about the regiment, and how proud we should feel, we now bore the exalted title of "gunner". There was more talk on these lines, about battles fought, honours won, and VCs awarded. No doubt these speeches were all an endeavor to cultivate a certain *esprit de corps* among the new gunners. Whether they did or not is hard to say so many years later.

By this time, it was creeping towards 11:00 hours, when, after a few words had passed between the major and the BSM, the troops were brought to attention. Sergeant Scott then stepped forward and announced, "There will now be an extended NAAFI break. Training will begin in earnest after lunch at 13:00 hours," followed by the order, "Troops... troops dismiss."

Fate is a difficult thing to define, but strange as it may seem, it was during this very first NAAFI break that I had the good fortune to meet two other 'C' troop members, fellows who became my erstwhile companions and true friends for the remainder of my military career. I will never understand how we three were thrown together, but on collecting a wad [a sandwich], and mug of tea at the counter, we gravitated to the same table. Right from the start, there seemed to be this sort of bond between us.

Ernest Beresford came from Burslem [one of the five towns that constitute Stoke-on-Trent, made famous in the books written by Arnold Bennett], approximately sixteen miles from my own hometown. With his elongated chin and cheeky grin, he was the double of Tommy Handley, the great comic star of the BBC wartime program ITMA [*It's That Man Again*]. He was a beautiful dancer, and a beaming smile coupled with a jovial and captivating personality made him very popular, not only with the other fellows, but also with the opposite sex. His romantic escapades were passionate and many, but somehow he always got away when things became a bit too serious.

Douglas Allsop, who came from Ilford on the eastern outskirts of London, was quiet, unassuming, and just the opposite of Ernie. Two or three months later, he disclosed to Ernie and myself that he had been raised in an orphanage [Dr. Barnardo's], and that he had no family or close relatives that he knew of at that time. Doug was one of the nicest fellows I have ever known and one could not help but like him.

Although our little trio came from very different backgrounds, we became very close friends, and throughout the next few years experienced many adventures together.

Wally Owen, from Selly Oak, Birmingham was another good pal I met soon after arriving at Shoeburyness. He was good humored, yet serious. He was intelligent, and determined to get a better education and advance in life. Whenever there was a spare minute or two, Wally would produce a book and was instantly lost in another world. He didn't always accompany our trio, but generally tagged along if we were going to a dance or cinema in

Gunner Wally Owen

Southend. Unfortunately, within a few weeks of reaching India, Wally was posted further east, while Ernie, Doug and myself traveled north, but more of that later.

One thing Wally was intent on losing was his 'black country' accent, which actually wasn't too bad, but as he pointed out, "Have you ever heard of anyone with a strong Birmingham accent being made chairman of a large corporation?" No, I hadn't, but then I didn't know any chairmen of large corporations.

I can only give an example of the awful local pronunciation by relating a joke. There are many Eli's and Enoch's in this large central industrial region of England, and so when Enoch meets Eli he inquires: —

"Wert yo bin ar Eli?" ["Where have you been, Eli?"]

"Ar bin fishin in t cut." ["I've been fishing in the canal."]

"D'yo ketch anyfin?"

"Ar, ar cote a whale."

"What yo do wif it?"

"Ar threwd it back in, cos it ad no spooks." ["I threw it back in because it had no spokes," the humour lying in that "whale" was the local pronunciation for "wheel".]

We four kept in touch for many years, even after the conflict, but like other wartime friendships, they gradually faded away. I sometimes wonder what happened to poor old Doug. One of the last letters I received from Wally Owen was from Cyprus, informing me that he had just been promoted to Regimental Sergeant Major, a position I'm sure he excelled in. He was ambitious, completely honest, a natural leader, and I have no doubt at all that he deserved the "step up". I feel certain that if he did decide to stay in the army, as he contemplated at one time, he would eventually attend an officers college training unit [OCTU].

Back to the story.

At the appointed hour, the two troops marched over to one of the gun sheds. Two six-pounder anti-tank guns were manhandled outside and positioned about thirty yards apart. The order then came for 'B' troop to gather around Bombardier Poole at the rear of one gun, and 'C' troop do the same around the other gun, with Sergeant Scott in charge.

The size of the gun was a surprise to all. Surely, I thought, this "dinky toy" would prove to be useless against a German tank, but the sergeant assured the group that it was a most lethal weapon. He related to the group how, at the beginning of the war, only ineffective two-pounder anti-tank guns were available. "It was," he said, "like shooting peas at a brick wall. Take it from me; this is a great little gun."

Six-pounder Anti-tank Gun

The trails, [legs], were opened up and gently lowered onto the tarmac. After giving a brief introductory description of the weapon, the new gunners were invited to inspect this piece of offensive hardware and ask questions.

One of the first questions asked echoed my own thoughts about German tanks. The answer given was that by the time we left Shoeburyness we would have full confidence in the weapon and its armour piercing ammunition. In addition, we would receive details and information on all enemy armoured vehicles, including where they were most vulnerable to attack.

After about two hours, the guns were trundled back into the shed, and the troop assembled in a room decorated with pictures and silhouettes of American, British, Italian and German tanks, self-propelled guns, and armoured cars. However, the slide illustrated lecture given was not about tanks, but all about the six-pounder gun. It's curved shield, [the top of which is not straight but undulating], the recoil system, firing mechanism, [primary and emergency], the breach, the sighting telescope, the "spades", range and velocity of the shot [the armour piercing projectile], and the different types of ammunition. At the end of the lecture, at around 16:30 hours, the gunners were marched back to the billets and dismissed for the day.

The few days left in that week were actually quite easy, but on the following Monday morning training became a great deal more concentrated and serious. The sequence of orders, stations and jobs of each member of the team had to be absorbed and practiced over and over again, until it became second nature. Dummy shells were repeatedly loaded and unloaded. We were also shown the procedure to be followed if a shell misfired, a problem that was to affect our team, and especially Gunner Gilbert, a few weeks later.

On the outskirts of the barracks, some old dilapidated buildings had been further knocked about to resemble a war damaged village. First we would go through the wrecked houses looking for booby traps. The most popular of these seemed to be the anti-personnel "book mine", so called because it was small and flat and could be inserted inside a modified book, or under an ornament. When one opened the book, or lifted the object, the damn thing would blow up.

We would also crawl along the street, prodding the ground with our bayonets, searching for those terrible Telle anti-personnel mines. This mine, when trodden upon, would eject upwards from its housing a small canister, which, at a height of four to six feet would explode, sending dozens of small steel balls in all directions. Once the "village" had been cleared of booby traps and mines, the next thing was to manhandle the gun through and over all the rubble, and position it in the best defensive and offensive position.

 Close by, there was a large "bomb crater", into which a gun would be lowered and teams had to extricate same. My first impression was that it couldn't be done, but of course, the army knew otherwise. By locking each wheel in turn, and swinging the gun through a series of maneuvers, and with the aid of ropes attached to the wheel hubs, there it was up, out and ready for action. The gun may have been ready for action, but the five members of the team were absolutely exhausted. The question that entered my mind was, "How the hell would a piece of artillery land up in a bomb crater?"

Interspersed among all this training on the guns were route marches, sessions in the gymnasium involving exercises with dummy six-pounder shells, square bashing, guard duties, lectures, fatigues, armoured vehicle recognition classes, tactics, and, of course, FFI medical examinations, or should that be "inspections". Why did we have to have route marches when we were supposed to ride into war on a Lloyd carrier?

As I have already stated, there are five men in a gun team. This is not strictly true, because there is, in fact, one extra person. He is the gun commander, generally an NCO. Immediately upon positioning the gun and before going into action, the gun commander would place himself out on the flank, choose the best target, and relay this information back to the gun team.

Meanwhile one of the gunners would take up a position on the opposite flank, with a Bren gun. His job was to pepper the target in the hope that the tank commander would close his visor, or perhaps, with a bit of luck, a bullet would find its way through a visor, thereby wounding or killing one of the tank occupants.

On the fourth week, the whole battery traveled to the firing range at Foulness. It was an apt name, for this was a flat image-less piece of coastal wilderness, upon which there was not one single tree. Foulness is a sort of semi-island, because when the tide flows in, it becomes separated from the mainland. Each team bounced along the few miles of road and bridges to the range in its own Lloyd carrier, towing a six-pounder. A Lloyd carrier is a tracked troop and ammunition transporter, designed especially for anti-tank guns.

The BSM was already there waiting to direct the guns to their respective sites. All pieces, [barrel plus breach], had to point out across the north sea. My team dismounted, unhooked the gun, manhandled it into position, opened the trails, and slammed the spades into the semi sandy ground, [the spades are supposed to restrict the gun from jolting backwards when fired]. Then, upon the order "detachment rear", the team fell in at the rear of the gun.

The ammunition used that day, we were told, would be "flatheads". It seems this particular shot does not travel as far out to sea as regular ammunition, but it did make one hell of a bang, something they forgot to tell us about. I couldn't see the sense in all this, unless a salvage crew was going to collect the spent shots. Perhaps a passing ship had been hit sometime. Who knows?

Bombardier Poole pointed out our particular target way out to sea and then called out, "Number off."

"One", "two", "three", "four", "five", we shouted.

The next order was, "Action stations."

Number 1 ran out to the right flank with the Bren, while the remainder took up their allotted kneeling positions around the breach. Number 5 passed a shell to number 4, who passed same to number 3, who loaded the missile into the breach, shouted, "On target," and then slapped number 2, [the layer or aimer, and firer of the gun], on the shoulder to signal the gun was loaded, and ready to fire. What happened next shook everyone to the core. The explosion was so great and unexpected I thought my head had come off. In addition to this, the little gun's wheels rose frighteningly about a foot into the air from the recoil, and rammed the spades even further into the soil. Startled by all this, 2, 3 and 4 jumped back in alarm, but managed to keep their positions.

With three rounds fired, it was then "detachment rear" again. "Is everyone okay," asked the Bombardier.

"Yes Bombardier," we all replied. Then someone asked, "But why didn't you warn us about the gun rebounding so violently, and how ear splitting the explosion would be?"

Another gunner inquired, "Why can't we have cotton wool for our ears?"

The answer was, "If you have cotton wool in your ears, how are you going to hear the orders?" So that was that! At this rate, we would all be stone deaf by the time the war ended.

The team stations were rotated, and the firing routine repeated until every gunner had experienced all stations.

The reader may recall that I previously mentioned a "misfire drill". Well, on our third station change we had a misfire. The breach was gradually lowered until the percussion cap could be seen. Each member of the team plus Bombardier Poole confirmed that the cap had been struck. The breach was carefully allowed to close, and after five minutes, this inspection was repeated. After another fifteen minutes, the Bombardier ordered the breach fully opened, and the shell carefully removed. Imagine my consternation, when he turned to Gunner Gilbert 524, and ordered him to take the shell three hundred yards inland and carefully place it on the ground, preferably in a trench, of which he said there were plenty.

Scared stiff, and with the shell cradled in my arms, I walked as fast as I could, at the same time being extremely careful not to trip or stumble. The missile appeared to get heavier with each successive stride, but at last, estimating I had gone far enough, a small trench was found, and with trembling arms, the shell was laid to rest. This done, like the clappers of hell, I covered two hundred yards in record time. Upon returning to the team, I was ribbed mercilessly, with remarks like, "Do you want to change your underwear?" and "You should have seen your face," and "Some people get all the luck." God was I glad it was all over!

On yet another visit to Foulness, Gunner Ogden was seriously injured. The whole barrel and breach, [the piece], is manually swiveled on its own central pivot, and when a change of target is ordered, number 3 jumps quickly to his feet, grabs hold of the breach, and training his eyes along the length of the piece, rotates same, until it is pointing in the direction of the new target. This done, he quickly takes his original position, shouts, "On target," slaps the layer's shoulder, who then concentrates his sights on the armoured vehicle.

In a previous paragraph, I referred to the emergency firing gear. This is a large button on the side of the breach that is used only when the primary firing mechanism is damaged in battle. On this occasion, the order from the flank was "target right". Immediately Gunner Ogden leaped to his feet, but in grabbing hold of the breach, he inadvertently hit the emergency firing button, and the gun fired. Luckily, his stomach was hard against the breach, so he was pushed rather than punched backwards by the recoil. Nevertheless, he was rushed to hospital with several broken ribs, and that is the last we saw of him.

At each new posting, there were always characters I would never forget, and one at Shoeburyness was Gunner Barratt. Barratt was a tall, scrawny, good hearted fellow from Bromsgrove, Worcestershire. Viewing him in the flesh, one could say without fear of contradiction, that he was definitely not a candidate for Tarzan. However, his enthusiasm for participating in everything and anything knew no bounds, and if the battery wanted a volunteer, he was their man.

Unfortunately, when poor old Barratt smiled, one could see he had several intermittently missing teeth, and this earned him the cruel nickname of "Graticule". This came about because the target-sighting telescope on an anti-tank gun has a horizontal line marked across the centre of the outer lens, and this is intersected at regular intervals with small vertical lines. These are known as 'graticules', and they allow the gun layer to compensate for the speed of a tank should it be crossing his line of fire. Hence, "Graticule Barratt".

Another was Gunner Connors. He came from Bethnal Green in the east end of London, only Connors pronounced it "Beffnil Grine". I had heard all about Cockney rhyming slang, but had never encountered it, until now. When he became excited, he would talk so fast in this strange and wonderful language that I, among most others, could not comprehend a word he was saying. Gradually, he would realize no one could understand this "foreign tongue", and change to more reasonable English. Strange as it may seem, I liked brash, cocky old Connors.

About five or six days after our arrival, I was looking over the serving counter into the kitchen, when I noticed an ATS cook who looked familiar. She in turn was looking at me, no doubt thinking to herself, "Who is this tall, dark, handsome, suave devil?" So after the meal, I wandered over to the counter, and after drawing her attention, inquired, "Do I know you from somewhere?"

"Well," she replied, "I've been trying to remember where I have seen you before. You don't happen to come from Stafford, do you?"

She turned out to be Dorothy, and her home was on the Lammascotes Road. After a long chat, she asked, "Have you had enough to eat? Do you want some bread, butter, and jam to make toast this evening? Save you spending money in the NAAFI." So saying, Dorothy slid away, and returned with a parcel of about six slices of bread *etc.*, with the warning, "Keep this to yourself, and don't let the parcel look too conspicuous." A couple of times a week this transaction would take place, and in the evening, Ernie, Doug and I would sit in front of the barrack room fire eating our toast, washed down with a mug of that horrible NAAFI "tea".

One evening, Bombardier Poole graced us with his presence, and one of the fellows inquired, "Were you stationed here at the time of Dunkirk, Bombardier?"

"Yes, I was," he replied shaking his head, "and what a bloody shambles that was," or words to that effect.

Ernie — "What do you mean?"

Poole — Well, to begin with, we had roughly thirty thousand men here. They were absolutely worn out, the poor sods. 90% of them had nothing but the uniform they stood up in, and that was in tatters. It was bloody terrible."

Ernie — "Thirty thousand men! Where on earth did they all sleep? Did they all have beds?"

Poole — "About a quarter of them had beds or pallets. The rest of the poor devils were in the gun sheds, in the church, in the library, in the NAAFI. They were all over the place, and just lay down were they could. Thirty thousand men and one 1914 Lewis gun among the lot of them. As for ammunition, it was estimated there was enough to keep firing for about fifteen minutes."

Some of my readers will no doubt smile and think I'm stretching things a bit, but I swear this is absolutely true. Those of you who were in Britain at that time know it to be true; so do those of you who have researched the calamitous situation the UK found itself in after the evacuation from Dunkirk.

Bombardier Poole continued, "During the day, groups would practice on this one solitary machine gun. Obviously, it couldn't be fired because the army was short of ammunition. Then at about 17:00 hours, our precious little gun, and all its ammunition, would be transported on a pick-up truck to the end of Southend Pier, where it was mounted in case the Germans decided to invade during the night." Southend Pier, which stretches out into the Thames estuary for nearly a mile, is reputed to be the longest pier in Britain.

"What about rifles?" Someone asked.

"Oh, we did have a few. About fifty, I think," replied the bombardier. "Morale was as low as it could get the first few weeks after the evacuation, but very gradually, things started to change. It was amazing to witness the transformation, from an army that had suffered a massive defeat, into a new fighting force, even if they didn't have any arms to fight with. Why Hitler didn't invade is beyond me. He could have walked in."

"There were infantry, tankers, medics, sappers, signalers, gunners; you name them, they were all here. Within a week, things began to be sorted out, and slowly moral began to improve. Every day batches of men would leave to join up again with their old units. The barracks became less crowded, the whole atmosphere gradually changed, and of course Churchill had become Prime Minister."

"During this time, a group of commandos arrived, and taught these survivors all about guerrilla warfare. How to make booby traps and weapons from every-day bits and pieces. How to disable a tank. That sort of thing. They were not going to give in without a fight. As Churchill declared, in one of his historic Sunday night radio speeches to the nation, `If you are going to go down, make sure you take a Narzee with you'." Churchill always referred to the Nazis as "Narzees".

Obviously there was a lot more, but the above is the gist of what Bombardier Poole related.

Many of the Commonwealth countries argued that King George VI and his government should move to Canada, but the king said he was not deserting his people, and the queen said she would not leave without the king, and Churchill defiantly stated he would fight the hun by throwing house bricks at him if all else failed.

It was at this time, to quote President John Kennedy, that Winston Spencer Churchill took the English language to war with his amazing famous fighting speeches. I quote one: "We shall fight on the beaches, we will fight in the streets, we will fight in the cities, we will fight in the hills. We will never surrender." Amazingly, it didn't come to that, but it was close thing. One cannot find the words to describe the determination of the nation not to give in to Hitler, and the electric atmosphere that hovered over the land in those fateful fourteen months when Britain fought on alone. Words are useless. Only those who were in Britain at that time know what it was like.

Once again, back to the story.

As March progressed into April, then May, the hours of daylight increased, and the weather became lovely and warm. In our spare time, we would lounge on our mini beach, or travel into Southend to attend a dance, or see a film.

On Saturdays, after forking out our pennies for a bus fare, meal, and ticket to the cinema, there wasn't much left to throw around for the rest of the week.

All during these months, by day and by night, great armadas of bombers passed overhead on their way to targets on the continent. At night, the drone of invisible hordes of Lancasters, Stirlings, and other heavy bombers of RAF Bomber Command could be heard, while in daylight hours, hundreds and hundreds of 8th USAF Flying Fortresses, Liberators, and Bostons produced an awesome sight. A few hours later, the sound of returning depleted squadrons made one look skywards again. Many were badly damaged, just about managing to limp home. These terribly battered planes with their brave young crews flew in so low that the damage was easily discernible. Wings half off, tails shot away, one and sometimes two engines gone. In addition, of course, there was the unseen dead and wounded on board the planes. They were terrible and memorable scenes to behold. To watch these scenes on film is one thing, but to actually witness them, and then try to find words to express one's thoughts at seeing this terrible carnage is quite another.

Everyone agreed, something big was going to happen soon, and it did on 6th June, 1944 — D-Day.

As the reader can imagine, the atmosphere on that legendary day was electrifying, to say the least. At every opportunity, someone would sneak off for a few minutes to listen to the radio, and bring back the latest news. Once or twice, the sergeant or bombardier would actually tell one of his gunners to slide off to the NAAFI to find out how the invasion was proceeding. The weather was awful, and one could not help thinking what a lousy day it was for such a massive and historic operation.

For we soldiers stationed on the last stop of a railway line, tucked into a corner of Essex, nothing seemed to be happening. On that day and the following days the most noticeable physical thing we observed was that all Allied planes now had three wide white stripes painted on the wings and fuselage, making them more easily recognizable.

About the third week in June, I received word from home that Bernard Concar, a fellow member of the 8th Stafford boy scout troop, had been killed in Normandy on 7th June. Because he and I belonged to the same scout group, he was a friend, but not a close friend. Nevertheless, it came as a terrible shock. I just couldn't believe it. Bernard was 19 years of age.

About three weeks before we were due to leave Shoeburyness, the troop was introduced to the new 17-pounder anti-tank gun, now coming off the assembly lines in ever-increasing numbers. Rumors had been going around that the regiment would be getting some of these latest weapons, so it wasn't a complete surprise when six were trundled out of the gun sheds. We already knew 17-pounders were being mounted on the new Cromwell tanks, and reports indicated it was a very effective weapon.

17-pounder, Anti-tank Gun

Now, this was a gun one could feel confident about! It was big, three times more powerful, and from all accounts deadly accurate. It still required a team of five, but the layer sat on a seat adjacent the piece, from which position he could rotate and/or elevate the piece by means of hand-wheels. Our confidence increased even more when we were informed of the newly designed ammunition called "armour piercing discarded sabot" — APDS.

For the next three weeks, every minute was concentrated on the new gun, because gunners had to be proficient before being passed on to the next and final phase of training. Tank recognition was placed on the back burner. Emphasis was directed entirely towards learning about the mechanics of the new weapon and whipping the existing teams into shape. The recoil system was very much different from the six-pounder. Whereas with our former gun the recoil was about 14 inches, this new steel monster flew back 36 inches, and until one got used to its ferocious action, it was quite unnerving. Just imagine yourself standing next to the breach block, and upon the layer pulling the trigger, this great mass of metal comes flying past your ear.

Compounding all this was the fact that the shells were one hell of a weight. They stood nearly three feet high and about five inches in diameter. All exercises in the gym now involved tossing dummy 17 pounder shells around.

Looking back, I don't know how I managed to hurl those great things about. In fact, I don't know how I did a lot of the things I did in those times. It's a wonder half the regiment didn't do themselves a great injustice, resulting in higher pitched voices.

As our time in this corner of Essex drew to a close, everyone was 100% certain that by autumn we would all be in the thick of the fighting on the continent, that is, if the invasion forces were not pushed back into the English Channel. The battle situation was very precarious.

Once more the weeks moved slowly by, and the question on everyone's lips was, "Where will we be going to next?" By the end of June, this question was answered. Conway in North Wales was to be our next base, and soon we would be on the move again, not as individuals this time, but as a whole battery. However, before this happened, a leave of 14 days was granted. Ration cards and railway tickets were issued, and I was going home for the first time, [except for the 36 hours granted from Kingston] in ten months.

Doug told Ernie and me that he would be spending most of his time in London, and we naturally assumed he was going home to Romford. It turned out he spent his leave at a YMCA in Kensington. If he had said something, he could have come home with Ernie or myself, but we didn't know then of his lonely circumstances. Poor Douglas!

As for myself, I was returning to my hometown a much-changed person from the one who left in October of the previous year, and I wondered what my friends and family would think of it all.

Those two weeks of leave seemed to go by like the wind. Everyone said how well and fit I looked, and my family could not believe how much weight I had put on. My mother fussed over me like an old hen, even to the point of putting a stone hot water bottle in my bed, even though it was summer. Mum wanted to know all about my friends and especially if I had got involved with any girls.

Old friends were visited and dances attended at St. Paul's Parish Hall, St. Pat's, and the Borough Hall. These places were full to capacity, especially after the pubs closed, with servicemen and women from all over the globe, the most numerous being the "jitter-bugging" Americans, throwing their money around, and getting all the girls.

There was a very famous saying at that time: "The Americans are over-paid, over-sexed, and over here." Be that as it may, I don't know what we would have done without them. Britain may have held out against the boche for one, two or even three years, but the war could never have been won without the immense amounts of arms and men the USA poured into the war effort. And of course, the massive Russian army was beating hell out of the Germans on the eastern front.

One had only to cycle around the outskirts of Stafford, places like Baswich and Beaconside, to witness the awesome sight of hundreds and hundreds of American trucks, tanks, jeeps, vehicles of all types, lined up in great long rows ready to be moved south and across the channel into Normandy. Moreover, this was just one of a multitude of such "parking lots" spread across the land. It's a wonder our little island didn't sink under the weight of it all.

The depressing part of my leave was seeing those small convoys of ambulances traveling from the railway station to the huge American hospital housed in Shugborough Park. It was an every-day occurrence, and it was heartbreaking to think that many of the more severely wounded GIs would never see their homeland again.

On the day I had to return to Shoeburyness, after my father and brother had left for work, my mother made sandwiches for her soldier son, all the time asking if he had got everything, and making me promise not to do anything silly. Then finally, after referring to the death of Bernard Concar, she broke down and wept. I didn't know what to do. I put my arms around her and held her close until she had settled down once more, then, as quickly as I could, I collected my gear together, gave her one last hug and kiss, and left the house. Under the circumstances, I thought it was the best thing to do. Even so, I could feel her eyes on me all the way up the road, until I turned the corner onto Wolverhampton Road. It meant a long wait for the train, but I just couldn't bear the sight of mum crying like that.

When the train eventually arrived, it was crowded as usual, dirty as usual, smelly as usual, yet somehow the atmosphere was not as usual. The passengers were more talkative and upbeat. The invasion force had not been pushed back into the English Channel, and now the Germans were the ones under attack from north, south, east, west, and from the air. It was just a question of time, everyone thought, before this dreadful war would be over. That was wishful thinking. It was to take another eleven months of bitter fighting before victory in Europe could be celebrated. Then the Allies had to tackle the Japanese.

Douglas Allsop greeted me at the entrance to Shoeburyness Railway Station. Arriving back early, he had reserved three beds for Ernie, me, and himself in the temporary quarters allotted. He grabbed my kitbag, and off we marched into the barracks. It was now Monday, and Doug had discovered the battery would be moving out on Wednesday morning.

Trains arrived from Fenchurch Street every hour, on the hour, so Doug and I strolled down to the station to meet Ernie. He wasn't on the first, but he was on the next. We dumped his equipment on the bed, and then headed over to the NAAFI for a wad and mug of tea. It was when we were relating what had happened on our leaves, that Doug told us he had spent his at Kensington YMCA. I felt terrible! Here I was carrying on about how nice my family and friends had been to me, and there was poor old Doug stuck in a hostel.

After explaining why he had spent his leave there, he then declared, "Ah, but I had a very interesting and fruitful leave. I visited the Dr. Barnardo's Home where I was raised, and through them, and through further inquiries at Somerset House, I managed to trace an aunt, a sister of my mother. I've written to her, and I'm hoping she'll reply, that is if she's still alive, and still resides in Newberry, Berkshire." Ernie and I were both sad and elated on hearing this news, and silently hoped he would not be disappointed. Life without a caring family was, to me, unimaginable.

At roll call on Tuesday morning, it was announced that the battery would be leaving on the 08:15 train. Breakfast would be at 06:00 hours, and the battery would fall in at 07:30 hours ready to march off to the station. Otherwise, the rest of the day was ours.

First, our trio made its way to the cookhouse, where we said our fond farewells to Dorothy, our supplier of toast and jam for the past twelve weeks. Then we tried, in vain, to find Bombardier Poole. Fortunately, someone told him we had been looking for him, and happy to say, he found us later that day. He was a good NCO, and he made our stay more pleasant than it might have been.

At the ungodly hour of 05:00 the next morning, ablutions were being performed and gear packed. On the way to the dining room, kitbags were loaded onto waiting lorries, and after breakfast, everyone was handed a package of sandwiches, a piece of cake, and an apple. This was supposed to sustain these young gunners' appetites until they arrived at Conway, estimated to be anywhere between 17:00 and 19:00 hours.

At the appointed hour, the troops formed up on the barrack square for a roll call, and a few minutes later the battery marched through the barrack gates toward the station and the waiting train. One good thing was that we didn't see our kitbags again until reaching the final destination. At Fenchurch Street Station, a small convoy of RASC lorries and buses provided transportation to Euston Railway Station, where the WVS and Salvation Army handed out mugs of tea and assorted fodder, followed by another roll call.

A few hours later I was pointing out to Doug and Ernie the English Electric factory where I had worked, and 25 Shrewsbury Road, the home I had walked away from just three days ago. I frantically waved from the window on the chance someone might see me. Alas, nobody did.

At the railway junction of Crewe, the good old WVS and Sally Ann were once again waiting with mugs of tea and goodies. While this was going on, many soldiers got off the train, but many more got on, some of whom would join our regiment at Conway. It seemed to take ages to get everyone sorted out, but eventually, the train clackerty-clacked its way over numerous tracks, as it changed direction to the west. Gradually, the scenery began to change once more. On the distant left, one could see rising hills, while now and then the sea came into view on the opposite side. Flint passed by, then the holiday towns of Prestatyn, Rhyl, Colwyn Bay, Llandudno Junction, until finally Conway came into view.

As it crossed over the river of the same name, and alongside the massive 13th century castle, the troop-train began to reduce speed. It dawdled through the small town, and about half a mile from the outskirts, left the main line and finally came to rest at the camp's own private makeshift station, [a long, roofless wooden platform], on Conway Morfa, about a mile outside of town. Morfa is the Welsh name for a stretch of sandy scrubland.

This was to be our new home for the next few weeks.

Chapter Five
Conway, North Wales

———⟨⟨⟨⟨⟨⟩———

A huge number of Nissen huts and other buildings had been erected on this stretch of wasteland known locally as Conway Morfa to accommodate our new unit, namely the 270th Anti-tank Regiment, commanding officer Colonel John Bacon MM. The camp was laid out in a series of small open-ended squares with eight Nissen huts, four on opposing sides of each square, and all parallel to the coastline. Administrative offices, gun and transport sheds, workshops, armoury, guard room, and the main gate lay to the north, while situated towards the middle of the camp, sat the dining rooms, showers, latrines, and NAAFI. I cannot exactly remember what lay to the south, but I think it was high sand dunes, and surrounding the whole area, right down and out into the water, was a tall barbed wire fence. Two hundred yards to the west, over gently inclined grass tufted sand, the Irish Sea lapped quietly at the shore, while to the east, across the railway line and main coastal road beyond, sheep dotted fields soon gave way to yellow mantled gorse hills, and then to heather blanketed mountains.

Alighting from the train, the new arrivals were greeted by several NCOs and officers, who invited the new arrivals to walk over to one particular square, form up, and await further instructions. These instructions, when announced, detailed who would be occupying each designated Nissen hut, and as names were called out in alphabetical order, it meant that "Graticule" Barratt, Doug, Ernie, and myself, would all be sharing the same billet once more.

However, this time there also happened to be another Gilbert in our billet, which for a few days caused a bit of a problem. When at roll call, Gilbert 524, [the usual way of addressing individual soldiers on parade], was called out there were sometimes, two responses. The cause of this confusion was that Jimmy's number was 924, and so as Jimmy was a couple of months older than I, it was resolved that he would be Gilbert "Senior", and I Gilbert "Junior". Eventually, after about a week, the "Gilbert" was dropped, and we answered to "Senior" and "Junior".

Gunners in Wales

Next day came the usual introductions, and yet more of those "welcome to the regiment" speeches. Strange as it may seem we were again in 'C' troop. The Bombardier's name was Barnes, and the Sergeant was a Cornishman by the name of Caulfield. He had this slow drawling way of speaking, and one of the fellows remarked that he sounded more like a Canadian than a native of England.

A medium height, thin, very thin, round steel bespectacled Lieutenant then stepped forward, and this proved to be our new troop commander Harvey, hereafter nicknamed "Tojo", for that is who he looked like. For all his looks, he turned out to be an excellent officer, and was popular with his men.

"From now on," Lieutenant Harvey announced, "all training will be on the 17-pounder anti-tank gun. All equipment will be blanco'd dark green, and brasses painted black. Training schemes, [exercises], of varying lengths of time will take place in the mountains, always ending at the firing range at Harlech, where mock actions with live ammunition will take place. Plus, there will be days when you will visit the Battle Inoculation Course in the mountains east of Llanfairfechan. During the last four weeks, but only when you are in camp, you will be required to carry your rifles everywhere. This includes the dining room, NAAFI, showers, and latrines. Everywhere, means just that — everywhere. This way, you will get to know the 'feel' of your rifle, so that even in the dark, you'll be able to recognize your own personal weapon."

He continued, "Lastly, during the 6th week of your stay, you will be informed where your next posting will be, and receive lectures and information related to that posting. This information is top secret, and must not be divulged to anyone, not even your own family. Remember, careless talk costs lives' and in this case it could be your own and your fellow gunners' lives that will be at stake. Let me make this perfectly clear. Anyone caught or even suspected of careless talk, even if you are only chatting amongst yourselves in some public place such as a pub, regarding this highly classified information, will be arrested immediately and charged under the official secrets act. — Do you all understand?"

"Yes sir," came the return chorus.

So there it was, and presuming we would be granted 21 days embarkation leave, it was now quite evident that within twelve to fourteen weeks these young gunners were bound for foreign shores, but where? Dark green blanco, and tarnished brasses could mean anywhere. Ernie said it sounded definitely like northern France or Italy. Doug thought it might be the Balkans. We were all wrong.

Colonel John Bacon, [nicknamed "Streaky"], was a career soldier steeped in the traditions and history of the Royal Regiment of Artillery. He would arrive at his Nissen hut office at exactly 08:00 hours, [plus or minus 30 seconds], every morning, and upon exiting his car would stand to attention and salute the six-pounder anti-tank gun parked outside the building. His chauffeur, staff, and office sentries also had to follow this traditional routine. "Remember," he would inform all and sundry within earshot, "the Royal Regiment of Artillery has no colours. The guns are our colours, and shall be treated with all due respect."

Streaky had made a name for himself in the Western Desert, commanding a battery of 25-pounder field guns. When confronted by German tanks he ferociously attacked them over open sights and destroyed or damaged many of them, so much so that the enemy withdrew to lick their wounds. Unfortunately, during this action, he was gravely wounded and had to leave the field of battle. For this heroism, he was awarded the Military Cross, one of the highest decorations in the British Army. After months in hospital, he was posted back to England, promoted, and placed in command of the 270th

Anti-tank Regiment.

Unfortunately, he was also an ardent Catholic, and as such, he made sure all personnel of that faith were marched to the Catholic church in Conway to attend Sunday Mass. Not only that, but after Mass he would sometimes inspect his men while all the parishioners looked on. He would then stand to attention by his car, and as we marched past, the order "eyes left" would be given, and the Sergeant would give a smart salute, which Streaky acknowledged with an equally smart salute. Naturally, on these occasions our best battle dress had to be worn. Why couldn't he have been a Methodist, Baptist, or C of E?

Colonel Bacon also had this gift for remembering faces, especially Catholic faces. He also had an eye for detail and noticed all sorts of minor infringements other officers would let go by. Field sports were yet another of his fads, and two weeks into our training there was a sports afternoon, when four batteries competed against each other. Naturally, Gunner Barratt was the first to volunteer from our troop and was duly entered for three events. Alas, poor old Graticule came hopelessly last in all three, but got the biggest cheers from the crowd. The colonel made a point of approaching Barratt, to congratulate him on a fine performance. I thought what a grand gesture this was.

On one of our many visits to Harlech, Streaky arrived to watch his gunners in action. He walked along the gun sites until he reached 'C' Troop, and after few minutes, asked Tojo to form "detachment rear". He inspected the line-up for a minute or two, then stepped forward declaring, "Aren't you Barratt, the athlete?"

"Yes sir," replied Barratt.

"Bloody fine show you put on last week. How are you enjoying the training here gunner?"

Again Barratt replied, "Very much so, sir."

"Bloody good show. Excellent. Keep up the good work." With that, he walked away, and Gunner Barratt was on cloud nine.

However, on another occasion, the Colonel was not to be so popular with 'C' Troop. Let me explain. A British soldier is issued with two battle dresses plus one set of denim fatigue wear. Obviously, you kept the best fitting battle dress for attending dances, visiting the cinema, or going on leave. The other, you're second best, you would wear on schemes and guard duty. At least, that's what we did. This time, when the Colonel inspected 'C' Troop, he stopped in front of one gunner and asked, "Is this your best battle dress gunner?"

"No sir," the hapless idiot soldier replied.

Streaky went berserk. "Why the bloody hell isn't it? Don't you know the guns are your colours? Don't you know you should always treat the regimental colours with the utmost respect by wearing your best battle dress? — Do you understand?" — Then, taking three or four strides backwards, he bellowed at the whole team in this manner —

"Do — you — all — understand?"

"Yes sir?" The troop replied in unison.

We were dumbfounded. This was ridiculous beyond words, even for the military. Just imagine going to a dance in a uniform smelling to high heaven of cordite. No girl would come near you. It was worse than having BO.

On those three or four day and night exercises, the only article of clothing you changed was your socks. You even slept in your battle dress. The bivouac sites along the way to the firing range were only rudimentary, equipped with washbasins, crude dirt toilets, and simple field kitchens. I suppose the army was trying to imitate actual combat conditions. Luckily, when at last we did arrive at Harlech there was always lots of hot water for showers.

The first night of the very first scheme, spent near the small town of Capel Curig, was yet another memorable occasion. 'C' Troop had been taking part in dummy actions all day long, and by nightfall, everyone was dead tired and as hungry as wolves. After being fed, the lads started to settle down for the night. It had been a lovely day, but as the sun went down, so did the temperature.

Army rain capes were designed in such a way, that by clipping two together they formed a small bivouac to give shelter for two soldiers. Ernie and I shared one, and after wrapping our fully clothed selves in our one blanket, we tried to settle down for the night. It was hopeless, trying to get comfortable on that hard and rocky ground. After a few minutes, I crept out, collected armfuls of bracken, and this I laid over the previously stone cleared patch and the hole I had knocked in the ground for my hip. The next thing I knew, Ernie, was by my side, and then several other gunners were up doing the same thing.

Next morning, these self-same gunners wanted to know if I knew any more tricks, so I told them about the hole for the hip. They had no idea how to take care of themselves in such circumstances. Next night, Doug, Ernie and myself made our bed under the Lloyd carrier, [against all rules], attaching the rain capes around the outside of the vehicle for protection against the inclement weather. It was a tight squeeze, but it worked. I also got them to dig a drainage trench around the carrier, in case of rain, which it did on later schemes. Once again, I owed a debt of gratitude to Bill Chesworth.

I don't think I have ever spent such cold and wretched nights in my whole life, as on those bleak Welsh mountains. How the army expected men to endure such conditions and then fight again next morning is beyond me, but they did. It's amazing what you can do when you have to.

Conway may be very different today, but then it was a very small, very respectable, very religious, and very dull little town. One gunner described it as "a cemetery with lights", except no lights were allowed because of the black-out. The narrow streets were lined with sombre looking houses of two shades of grey. The tiled roofs were a sort of blue-grey slate, and the outer walls of a softer, lighter grey. They didn't look too bad when the sun shone, but looked drab and miserable when the rain transformed the greys to black and near black. Each house had a nearly identical lace curtain half way up the front window, blocking the view of any "nosey parker" wanting to see into the front parlour. A few also had large aspidistras at the window.

There were a few shops, a canteen, and that was about it. Evenings were quiet to say the least, but on Sundays, it was totally comatose. The only busy places were the churches and chapels, of which there were many. Nothing moved. No shops, no pubs, no cinema, no buses — nothing. Fortunately, the trains still ran, so we would board one to Llandudno Junction, and from there transfer to the shuttle train into Llandudno itself. Llandudno, [pronounced Shlandidno], is a seaside resort, about three times the size of Conway, but remember, this was religious Welsh Wales, so even here everywhere closed down on the Sabbath.

Saturday night was the big night out. There were a couple of good dance halls in Llandudno, the better one being right next door to the Odeon Cinema. Both had good little bands, but the one near the Odeon had a better floor and more girls. Alas, we couldn't date any because troops stationed away from the town had to leave at about 22:30 hours in order to get back to camp by 23:59 hours. Later than that and you were placed on a charge. The first time we attended a dance, we got hopelessly lost in the black-out when trying to find our way back to the railway station, but eventually we made it.

On two occasions, the battery spent a very "pleasant" day at the Battle Inoculation Course, and it was on the latter visit that Gunner Gilbert was "wounded", so henceforth the lads referred to it as "the Battle of Llanfairfechan". Actually, the course was situated in the mountains to the east, and about half way between that village and a tiny hamlet with the equally unpronounceable name of Penmaenmawr.

"Full battle order" means a soldier is equipped with his small pack, ammunition pouches, gas mask, bayonet, rifle, steel helmet, and a few other luxury items. One of these latter items is a thing called a field dressing, a great anti-septic treated wad attached to a lengthy wide bandage. This sealed package is always kept in a pocket high on the left leg of one's battle dress.

Time has erased from my memory much of the wonderful entertainment the army provided on those days, but I do, and always will remember the withering machine gun fire and mortar barrage.

'C' Troop, in line abreast, alternatively marched, charged, and crawled across the mountainside with bullets flying by just above our heads. At the same time, mortars laid down a screen of high explosive and smoke bombs. All one could think about at the time was, "I hope those swine know what the hell they're doing, and trust I'll get to the other end without need of a toilet." After what seemed to be an eternity, but was in fact only about a couple of hours, we came to a welcome rest. "Thank god that's all over," I thought, but soon learned that what we had endured was only the supporting act to the main event.

After a short break, the troop was once again crawling across three to four hundred more yards of mountainside to the banks of a fast flowing mountain stream. Two at a time, we rolled off the bank into roughly four feet of icy cold water, and being only 5 feet 6 inches tall, the swirling mass rose to my manly chest. With Lee-Enfield rifles held above our heads, we struggled against the current, and all this time live ammunition seemed to be coming at us from all directions. For about 10 minutes the gunners fought the stream, bullets, and bombs until they reached a backward sloping 20-foot high cliff and this had to be assaulted.

Everything went fairly well on the first trip, even though it was a horrifying experience, and while everyone was better prepared for our second and final visit, all did not go according to plan. This is what happened.

'C' Troop completed the first part okay. These brave gunners, with bullets and bombs screaming overhead, crawled across and up the mountain, and once again rolled into the rushing, freezing cold stream. Again we fought against the torrent, reached, and scaled the cliff. At last, all of 'C' Troop were at the top, where we all collapsed in a state of utter exhaustion. One of the fellows looked at me and asked, "What's all that blood on your battle dress?" It was only then I realized that blood was pouring down my left cheek. After inspection by Sergeant Caulfield, someone was ordered to wrap a field dressing around my head, and so, with this great wad in place, we

71

prepared for the march back to Conway.

It turned out I had been wounded by a mortar bomb, and a piece of shrapnel was lodged to the left and below my left eye. Another inch and I would have lost the use of that eye. For some reason the doctor was unable to remove this bit of ironmongery, and it was not until 1956 that I was relieved of the memento. It looked like a small washer.

These teenage bedraggled soldiers must have looked like a pack of drowned rats as they marched through Penmaenmauwr. At the side of the road, a group of older women just stood and stared at these stalwart, rugged, soaking wet warriors. As the troop passed by them, one old lady looked straight at me, and turning to the other women exclaiming, "Poor little bugger." Ernie Beresford, upon hearing this, called to them, "He'll do anything for a laugh, missus."

With so much activity going on, the first four weeks flew by. Wherever we went from now on, our rifles accompanied us. In the dining room, all rifles were lined up against the wall, and as many looked exactly alike, some confusion reigned after a meal.

It was some time in the second week of August that I received the heartrending letter from home telling me that Eric Mansell, an infantryman in the South Lancashire Regiment, had been killed on 2nd August in the battle for Caen in Normandy.

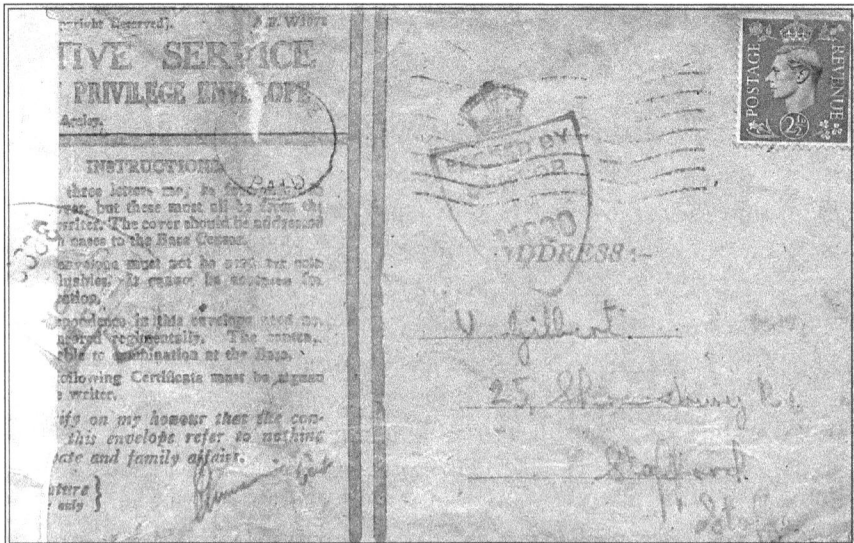

Eric Mansell's Last Letter

Private Eric Mansell

I was devastated and in a complete state of shock. I had never experienced such feelings before. He was my very best friend, and had been since we met at St. Austin's school at age five. We were closer than brothers, if that is possible.

Tears began to roll down my cheeks, so I hastily left the hut and made my way to the latrines, where I sat, reread the letter, and silently sobbed. It couldn't be true. Your best friend was not supposed to get killed. It was all a mistake. Surely, in a few days time another letter would arrive saying it was all wrong and that he was still alive and well. Yet in my grief-filled heart, I knew it must be so. He was my age, nineteen.

The terrible sadness would not leave me, and that night, in the darkness of the Nissen hut, I silently cried again. What a terrible waste of life. Eric was good looking, generous to a fault, musically talented, and a load of fun to be with. No more would we walk over Castle Fields together. Never again would we cycle out to Sherbrook Valley. Attending the dances at St. Pats or the Borough Hall was now a thing of the past. We went everywhere together. We were inseparable. He was a wonderful pal, and even to this day, when I think about him, like this very moment, tears begin to fill my eyes.

Who would be the next "Cherry Pit" camper to be killed? Would it be me?

Lol Dowd's ship had been torpedoed off the North Cape of Norway while escorting a convoy to Murmansk in Russia. Luckily, and against all odds, he had been quickly plucked from those sub-zero waters, but was confined to a Russian hospital for three months.

Paddy Pate, the story goes, had been left for dead on the beaches of Dunkirk, but was also miraculously saved by, of all people, one of his Cherry Pit friends, Len Preston. What a strange and wonderful coincidence. Over three hundred and fifty thousand men on those beaches, and he was carried on board a rescue boat by one of his fellow 8th Stafford Rover Scouts. Machine gun fire from a screaming German Stuka aircraft had ripped his back to pieces. After a year or more in hospital, he was found to be unfit for further service, and discharged from the army.

The Cherry Pit mentioned above was the pre-war and wartime permanent campsite of the 8th Stafford Boy Scouts, at Shelley's-the-Beacon farm on the outskirts of Stafford, and it was here that my companions and I spent practically every weekend during those far off, never to return, summers.

The sixth Monday arrived, and it was announced that the assembled battery would shortly be sailing for the Far East. No definite destination, just, "You will shortly be sailing to the Far East." The major continued, "For obvious reasons, you will not be issued with tropical gear until you arrive at the transit camp on the other side of the world, wherever that may be. On the day of departure, all troops will be allocated two bandoliers of .303 ammunition, for which you will be held responsible until handed in to the armoury at the overseas transit camp. I am not at liberty to tell you where your initial posting will be, but I can tell you, your final destination will be with the Fourteenth Army in Burma."

"During the next two weeks, all of you will be receiving inoculations against some of the diseases encountered in that part of the world. You will also receive lectures and see films of what you may encounter in the countries you will be visiting. Lastly, let me reinforce the statement made to you earlier by Lieutenant Harvey. All this information is top secret. Do not speak to anyone about your posting, not even your family, because as the poster declares, 'Careless talk costs lives.' Any reckless slip of the tongue could place the safety of yourself, your comrades, and the convoy in jeopardy. Have you all got the message?"

"Yes sir," came the reply.

In fact, over the next two weeks many messages were received. At one lecture we were informed, "Just because a Burmese lady gives you a lovely smile does not mean she wants to climb into bed with you. And remember VD is very prevalent in these countries." At the same time, we were shown horrifying pictures, in glorious technicolour and great detail, of victims' "paraphernalia" showing these nasty afflictions. It certainly put the fear of God into me I can tell you.

One film depicted a beautiful river scene — graceful palm trees, exotic flowers, rippling waterfall, and with lilting music being played: it all looked so peaceful, and idyllic. Then the narrator broke in, adding his own expletives, but concluded by saying, "— however, let us follow this river upstream."

Around the bend, some women were doing their laundry and washing babies, while nearby the village drain was emptying foul looking effluent into the river. Further on, a herd of buffalo were observed dropping their excrement into the water, and a short time later a man was seen urinating from the bank. There were more episodes like these, but those four particularly come to mind. There were also films and lectures on malaria, dysentery, and other delightful diseases.

These lectures and films, although very brutal and shocking, certainly got the message across. It certainly made my sex-mad comrade, Gunner Beresford take notice. He couldn't get over some of the pictures depicting patients afflicted with various types of VD, especially one, which was particularly ghastly.

On the last Wednesday afternoon of our training, the troop lined up to be handed three week's pay, railway tickets, leave passes, ration cards, and a piece of paper once more warning about careless talk. Being paid in the army is done to a special ritual. The troops form up, the order is given to "open order — march", and when the name Gilbert 524 is called, Gilbert 524 smartly comes to attention, marches up to the table, behind which sits the Troop Commander and Army Pay Corps Sergeant. Coming to a foot slamming halt and standing to attention, Gunner Gilbert salutes the officer with his right hand and receives his pay with his left. Then, after another smart salute, and an equally smart about turn, he marches back to his original position in the ranks.

Upon being dismissed, at about 15:00 hours, the lads raced off to the armoury, made out and tied labels to the trigger guard of their rifles, and handed in same for storage until their return. Back at the billet, kit was packed ready for tomorrow's journey.

Next morning, after breakfast and handing in blankets *etc.* the fellows boarded the train specially scheduled to stop at the camp's own rickety wooden station platform. It seemed to stop at every village and town on its way to Crewe, where we all went our different ways — Ernie to Stoke, Doug to Newbury, Berkshire, and myself to Stafford. Happily, Doug did get a reply from his long lost aunt, who invited him to spend his leave there. I am also happy to report that the reunion proved to be a great success, ending with the offer of a home when he returned from the war. How could anyone not like Doug?

Home for three weeks, twenty one days, of which some were happy and some very, very sad. Then it would be goodbye to family and friends for God knows how many years, or even if I would be one of the lucky ones to return to the fold. What will be, will be!

For servicemen stationed in the UK, leave is generally seven or fourteen days, but for embarkation leave one is granted an extra week, so as soon as you mention you are on three weeks leave, people immediately know you are going overseas.

I did all the usual things, like visiting and saying goodbye to friends, and attending dances at all the old haunts. The saddest visit was to see Eric Mansell's mother. She threw her arms around me, and cried and cried, and within a very short time, I'm afraid I too broke down. She hung on to me and would not let me leave. It was awful. At that point, I would have gladly slaughtered a hundred Germans, with not a trace of remorse.

The last few days were particularly difficult, and I warned my brothers and sister not to mention Eric Mansell or Bernard Concar, [the two friends who had been killed in the Normandy landings], when my parents were around. I could see my mother was close to tears, even though I kept assuring her that I would be all right. On the last day, she placed around my neck a lovely new rosary, blessed by Father Moore of St. Austin's church. The air was tense with emotion as I left home, and again I could feel my mother watching me as I made my way along Shrewsbury Road on my way to the station.

And so, after twenty-one days we returned to Conway, but this time we were housed in an old school close to the camp railway station. On day one, we retrieved and cleaned our Lee-Enfields, otherwise we just sat around and talked or visited the NAAFI. When nothing happened for a week, we all began to get restless. Time dragged and was mostly taken up with marches down to Llanfairfechan and back, or another of those lovely talks about tropical diseases, and there was one last FFI. Then, out of the blue, at lunchtime, the order came to pack our gear, keep one blanket, [mine was a Canadian Army blanket, which I still have], hand in the other two, and assemble at the camp station at 19:00 hours.

The troops lined up on the platform, and then, after one last roll call, boarded the special train that would take us to we knew not where. From bits of information gathered, it was obvious our first destination was India, but from which port the troopship would depart, was anybody's guess.

I suppose it must have been about 19:30 hours when the train slipped away from the station, and we said our farewells to Conway. More troops were picked up at Colwyn Bay and Rhyl, and as darkness fell, the guesswork began as to where we were heading. Liverpool and Birkenhead were the most popular choices, but when the train headed north after leaving Crewe, everyone gave up.

As mentioned previously, the problem was, ever since Dunkirk, sign-posts and nameplates had been removed everywhere, from roads, entrances to towns, post offices, and stations, so when the train came to a halt at around 22:00 hours, no one had a clue where we were. Another problem was the lack of light due to the black-out regulations. The shielded ceiling light inside the carriage had been painted blue, so illumination was practically nil, while outside ghost-like figures, wheeling trolleys around, could scarcely be seen.

Mugs of tea, cheese rolls, and other refreshments were provided by the Army Catering Corps, [no civilians this time], who hinted we were near Wigan. An hour later, the train, with its human freight, moved gently off once more. After demolishing the food, passengers tried to sleep, but it was almost impossible bunched up together like that. Some stretched out in the corridor.

On through the black of night our conveyance progressed, sometimes slowing to a crawl, sometimes stopping all together. As dawn broke, the troops found themselves passing through heavily populated and industrial areas, until eventually screeching brakes brought the train to a halt at the docks in Greenock alongside the River Clyde.

Chapter Six
Men of Harlech

Before I describe our voyage, however, there are a few stories that I would like to share about the training schemes and the village of Harlech,

For those who may be unfamiliar with this part of the British Isles, Harlech lies on the coast of Wales about eighty miles due north of Swansea, as the crow flies, but probably twice that amount by those narrow, twisting, up-hill and down-dale country roads. It's a small, pretty village whose main attraction is its large forbidding castle, built by King Edward I sometime in the 13th century, although it is perhaps better known because of the warriors who inhabited this area in that far distant past, and who are immortalized in the famous Welsh folk song, "Men of Harlech".

Some people will tell you that the only difference between winter and summer in this region of the British Isles is that the rain in summer is warmer. Fortunately, the summer of 1944 was to prove this to be somewhat untrue. To be quite honest, I cannot remember what the month of July was really like, but August was full of sunshine and soft, balmy, sea scented breezes, and it was in August that this particular incident took place.

Why was it, I wondered, did we always finish these exercises with a mock battle on the Morfa, 100 to 150 feet below the imposing structure of Harlech Castle, but that was always the case. Batteries of the 270th Anti-tank Regiment, Royal Artillery, would start off from Conway, for three to five day schemes, in which we young, khaki clad, steel helmeted, devil-may-care warriors would take part in make believe actions all through these Welsh mountains. Not a single live shot was fired. Because of this situation, and to make it more realistic, when one comedian in my gun team suggested that when the order to fire was given we should all shout, "Bang!" in unison, we all readily agreed, and so it was that cries of, "Bang, Bang, Bang!" reverberated throughout these rugged mountains. I thought to myself, "When we go into action, the Third Reich will never be able stand up to this sort of punishment".

I could just imagine a frightened Adolf Hitler sending a message to his generals saying, "The 270th Anti-tank Regiment is coming, therefore we must send two thousand reinforcement 'Bangs' to the front, or Germany will lose the war." Little did he know, we had more "Bangs" than he did, thank God!

A Morfa, for those not conversant with the Welsh language, is a flat piece of wasteland, and in the case of Harlech, it stretched for about two miles along the coast, and lay between the castle and the Irish Sea. It was here, when we eventually arrived, that real action with real ammunition took place.

Harlech Castle

Most times these schemes were quite enjoyable during the day, but at night it was miserable, trying to keep warm and snatch a few hours' sleep. We were free of the army camp, the scenery was beautiful, and people would wave to us as we passed through small towns and villages with such unpronounceable names such as Trawfsynnydd, Llanfiangel-y-traethau, and Llanrwstand, plus, there was always lots of good-hearted banter. That is most times! Mishaps did happen, sometimes with tragic consequences.

Once, on one of those very narrow single lane mountain roads, half a dozen girls were sitting on top of a stone wall, waving and exchanging friendly remarks with the young soldiers. Suddenly, one of them was seen to fall under the wheels of a lorry towing a 17-pounder anti-tank gun. By the time the convoy had halted, it was too late, and the poor girl was dead. It appears she had been swinging her legs out from the wall, when her foot caught a mudguard, and she was dragged under the wheels of both the lorry and the trailing gun. Five minutes before, my own troop had passed by them, so we didn't hear about the terrible tragedy until we stopped to camp for the night. The lads in the tow-piece had seen it all close up, and were in a complete state of shock, especially one 18 year old who was sent to hospital.

Another fatal accident occurred on the steep, winding narrow road connecting Harlech village to the Morfa below. Locals claimed it was the steepest hill in Britain, which 50 years later I found to be true. This is what happened.

The regiment had a battery of M10 self-propelled guns. These are Valentine tanks on which the turret has been replaced with a field or howitzer gun, and because these monsters are tracked weapons, they travel to where the action is on huge transporters. On this particular day, a transporter was climbing the above precarious road, when the driver tried to change down into a lower gear. He failed to accomplish this, and after much grinding of gears the whole combination stopped, then started to reverse slowly down the hill. As this loaded vehicle gained speed, the driver kept trying to get into gear and also applied the brakes in an endeavour to stop its downhill progress. Suddenly the gear was found and the transporter shot abruptly forward. Unfortunately, the transporter's load still wanted to go backwards, and as the cables holding the M10 in position fractured, the self-propelled gun slid off the back and over the cliff, coming to rest on the Morfa below. Even more unfortunate, was the fact that two gunners were sitting on the M10 at the time, and both were killed. Travelling as passengers in this fashion was against the rules, but then, we all broke the rules one time or another.

Before continuing with my story, I must describe the drill carried out by a gun team when going into action, and ask you to try and visualise this most dramatic scene.

A 17-pounder anti-tank gun team comprises of five men. The gun commander and No 1 man, armed with a Bren gun, take up a position on the flanks. The No 2 man is seated to the side of the breach, and it is he who sights on to the target and fires the gun. No 3 loads the shell into the breach, and stands right behind No 2. Directly in front of No 2 is an aperture in the shield of approximately 4 inches by 8 inches long, in the middle of which is mounted a telescope through which the gun layer, No 2, can zero in on the target. Now, when the gun commander orders "Target left," or whatever the case may be, No 2 moves his head out of the way and starts frantically turning a hand-wheel to bring the gun onto the target. As soon as No 2's head is out of the way, No 3 jumps to his feet, looks through the aperture, and as the tank comes into view shouts, "On target." Immediately upon hearing this, No 2 returns his eye to the telescope and concentrates on the target.

After all that, here is where this epic military episode really begins.

On this particular occasion Gunner Gilbert just happened to be No 3 on the team. The order came from the flank, "Target left," and No 2 immediately ducked his head out of the way, at the same time turning the hand-wheel to traverse the barrel of the gun. Gunner Gilbert promptly jumped up and stared through the aperture. The dummy tank came into view from the left, moved smoothly across the aperture and started to disappear to the right. The trouble was, Gunner Gilbert, for some unfathomable reason, could not remember the correct command to stop the gun progressing past the target, so as the tank proceeded to disappear from sight, in desperation he hit No. 2's shoulder and shouted, "Whoa, whoa, whoa!"

Alas and alack, at this inopportune moment, 'C' Troop's commander, Tojo [Lieutenant Harvey], happened to be watching and just about went bananas. "Stop, stop, stop!" he cried and ordered the team to fall in at the rear of the gun. In turn, he asked each one of us to explain all the different commands, and then turned to Gunner Gilbert with the question, "What is the correct order when the tank comes into view?"

I smartly replied, "On target sir."

"Right," said Tojo, "Now go back and do it correctly."

At the end of the day's action, hungry and tired, the gunners fell into three ranks and proceeded to march back the half mile or so to our billets. As we arrived outside the Nissen huts, Tojo shouted the order "Troop — troop halt, Gilbert w-h-o-a," and the whole troop broke up with laughter.

Even to this day, my wife, and friends who know the story, still call after me "Whoa — Gilbert Whoa," if I am rushing on or tackling a project too energetically.

About two months later, about 50% of the 270th Anti-Tank Regiment were posted to all different parts of the world. Some went to the Middle East, some, including Gunner Gilbert 524, to the Far East, and some, no doubt, were bound for northern France. When I look back on those days, I often wonder how many of those young men survived that terrible war, and if so, what became of them and where are they now?

Chapter Seven

The Johann de Witte

A journey, in our case a voyage, has to start somewhere, and ours began at the Scottish port of Greenock. Quite honestly, I do not think any of the bleary eyed, numb limbed, drowsy troops, could have cared less where they were. It could have been Liverpool, Southampton, Cardiff, or Timbuktu. They were just happy to have reached the embarkation port, get off the train and its cramped, stuffy conditions, stretch their aching limbs, and breath in some fresh air.

With all the cranes, derricks, and warehouses, the area could hardly be described as attractive, but then I suppose that applies to all dockyards, and with everyone feeling miserable after the long tedious journey, the cold chilly morning did nothing to improve matters.

Around 06:00 hours we wearily gathered our gear, fell in alongside the troop train, and after yet another roll call, trudged over the rows of railway lines and boarded a waiting ferry boat. One idiot gunner didn't realize it was a ferry, exclaiming, "Surely we're not going all the way to India on this thing?" Someone told him not to be so bloody stupid or words to that effect.

In a very few minutes, bells clanged, orders were shouted, ropes cast off, and the ferry, with its captive payload, slowly pulled away from the dockside. Some of the dock workers just stood and watched, while others waived goodbye and shouted, "Good luck lads!" The little boat churned its way downstream for a few miles, gradually leaving the city behind, before finally mooring alongside our troopship.

One by one, the gunners struggled up the narrow unsteady gangway, where an orderly was handing out cards indicating the space each soldier would occupy for the journey. Another orderly handed out three "Active Service Privilege Envelopes". These were for last letters to loved ones and friends, until we reached the transit camp in India. On the front of the envelope was a declaration stating that your letter did not contain any information that may be of use to the enemy, and this, one had to sign. Even so, army censors opened all these letters, and anything questionable was blanked out with a dark blue pencil.

The censor's blue pencil actually became part of every day wartime language. For instance, if ladies were present, and one wanted to answer a question, using a vulgar or swear word, one might reply, "I'm not 'blue pencil' well going to do that," or "Not 'blue pencil' likely," or "get 'blue pencil' stuffed.

So down into the bowels of the ship we descended. At each deck level there was someone who would look at your berth card and direct you even further down. When Ernie, Doug and myself finally located our berths, we just couldn't believe it. There was even less room here than at the infamous Manningham Lane barracks. This wasn't a troopship; it was a floating sardine tin.

The *Johann de Witte* was a 10,500-ton Dutch passenger liner that had managed to escape from the Germans, and had since been converted into a troopship. It's odd, but at my school, St. Patrick's, it was compulsory to read *The Black Tulip* by Alexander Dumas, in which Johann de Witte, a Dutch patriot, is one of the main characters, and here I was boarding a ship named after him.

On our designated deck, long mess tables had been fitted, over which hung rows of hammocks, each labeled with a row and place number, and in each of these string and canvas beds lay a life jacket. Here, one was supposed live, eat, and sleep. I can't even guess at the number of bodies that were on this and other decks, and it was quite scary to think that if ever the ship did receive a hit, only a very lucky few would scramble up on deck and, with a lot more luck, survive. Comments about the accommodation, and the War Office, were so vicious the air turned blue. Kitbags and other gear was stowed behind nets along the side of the ship, while rifles, bayonets, and our two bandoleers of 303 ammunition were safely deposited in the armoury.

By this time, I felt shattered, so after a surprisingly good breakfast, and much difficulty, I tried out the hammock, and fell fast asleep. Next thing I knew, Doug was awakening me with the news that all troops were to muster on deck with their life jackets. It was pandemonium. The troops milled around aimlessly, until directions came over the Tanoy system regarding which troops were to collect at which action station. Once the confusion was sorted out, and soldiers were at their correct station, a sermon followed regarding what to do in case of attack, and the correct way to wear a life jacket, which must be carried at all times.

"Each day," the voice continued, "all officers and men will assemble at 10:00 hours for roll call and notification of ship's orders for that day. Smoking is prohibited at all times below deck, and on deck after sunset. A lit cigarette can be seen over a long distance on a clear night. Anyone found disregarding these orders will be severely dealt with."

Lastly, a tablet of salt water soap, [useless], was distributed to each soldier, and that was that for the day, apart from getting together for meals.

About a third of the way from the bow, on the port side, 'C' Troop's station was in quite a good location, because it was very handy to the stairwell to our deck. Later, in a few days' time, we would make this our permanent residence for the remainder of the trip.

Johann de Witte

Meals were very much better than expected, especially the freshly baked bread, which was delicious. This compensated, in a small way, for the cramped conditions. With everyone seated, table, or row letters were called, and that row would report to the small galley to collect their meal. This routine was repeated daily, except the row letters would advance by one each day, so on the first day table 'A' was first in line, next day table 'B' was first and so on. It worked quite smoothly.

That first night, the majority turned in early, and soon all one could hear was the snoring, moaning and groaning of exhausted soldiers. Unfortunately, some could not get comfortable in their hammocks and eventually made their bed on the hard mess table below. Because the ship lay at anchor in the River Clyde, this was okay, but a bed on the table after reaching the open sea was quite out of the question.

Early the next afternoon, our 32-day "luxury cruise" really began. The *Johann de Witte* slowly made its way down river, and although everyone clambered up on deck to take what, for some, would be a last look at their native land, the ship was strangely quiet. As myself and my two pals leaned on the rail looking at the shore, Ernie, for once, became very serious, and posed the question, "Do you think we will ever see England again?" That was something no one could predict, and that question seemed to draw us closer together. "My god," I thought, "I might be one of those not coming back."

Until this time, it had all been a big game. Racing around the countryside, towing a big gun, firing at dummy tanks, waving at the girls as we passed through picturesque villages, camping out in beautiful Welsh countryside. Now, upon hearing Ernie's comment, I abruptly realized the games were over, and we were really off to war. It shook me to think of all the perils that might lie ahead, and I suddenly felt like a coward. I didn't want to die, or lose my sight or an arm or a leg. I suppose Eric Mansell, Bernard Concar, and the thousands of young men who launched themselves upon the beaches of Normandy, had similar thoughts going through their heads.

Douglas broke into my thoughts with, "What's the matter?"

I quickly replied, "Nothing. Just thinking," and so pushed it all to the back of my mind. What will be, will be!

Our troopship gradually caught up with other assorted vessels also moving steadily downstream, and shortly, upon sailing out into the Irish Sea, took up their respective positions within the main convoy and its naval escort. Our little trio, even though we were extremely weary, stayed on deck until about 22:00 hours, not wanting to descend into that military battery pen. Over on the right [sorry, starboard side], lights appeared, so that must have been the coast of Eire, the Irish Republic, who, of course, were not at war with Germany.

That second night, gently swinging in my hammock, I tried to figure out the best and quickest way of getting to the stairwell and out of this steel canister, should anything drastic happen. Everyone else, no doubt, was doing the same thing.

Next morning, all one could see was the sea and the bobbing ships making up the convoy. It was not a big convoy; I suppose there may have been about twelve to fifteen vessels in total. Destroyers and frigates were positioned around the perimeter, and I wondered if my friends Lol Dowd or Ron Eley were on any those "Men of War".

The group of ships appeared to be moving rather slowly, but obviously the speed of the convoy was the speed of the slowest ship, but what a lovely target we made. As one gunner remarked, "I can swim faster than this." Actually the ships were moving faster than we realized.

Next morning, after roll call, the Tanoy voice informed the troops that fifty prisoners were also on board, and therefore a small part of the forward deck would be out of bounds between 14:00 and 16:00 hours each day so they could get some exercise.

They turned out to be Indian deserters, ex-prisoners of war of the Italians who had been persuaded by members of the INA, [Indian National Army], to switch sides and fight against the British. Commanded by Chandra Bose, this army had its headquarters in Japan, and these poor, gullible Sepoys believed that when the Axis Powers had won the war their country would be granted immediate independence. Now they were being returned to their homeland to face courts martial for desertion and treason. Sad as this may appear to be, I wish to point out that all Indian servicemen and women were volunteers, and at that time the Indian army alone numbered over two million.

Chandra Bose did not belong to any branch of the Indian forces, but had been a long-time advocate for Indian independence from Britain. To this day, his disappearance after the surrender of Japan is still a mystery. The Japanese reported that he had died in a plane crash on Taiwan, but neither the British nor American intelligence services could confirm that a plane of any sort had crashed where the Japanese said it did. Others believe he became a monk and died peacefully in the 1980s. This mysterious monk, it is rumored, was secretly cremated in the middle of the night, by the light of a single motor bike, and that acid was poured over his face, in case someone should recognize him.

Back to the *Johann de Witte*.

An hour later, there was a "Whoop, whoop, whoop" over the Tanoy, and a call for action stations. Soldiers scampered hither and thither, bumping into one another, trying to reach their allotted stations. After roll call had been completed, the voice announced, "This has been a practice exercise. The time taken was not too bad, but must be improved. The next time, it may be the real thing."

For the first two days, many of the passengers did not eat a thing, and many were terribly seasick, including yours truly. Death was near at hand, I thought, but by the third day my stomach had got accustomed to the roll of the ship and gradually, very gradually, settled down. It was common knowledge that the Bay of Biscay had a reputation for being rough, so of course nobody was looking forward to that portion of the journey. However, when the convoy passed through this area, it was surprisingly calm.

The Rock of Gibralter

On the fourth or fifth day, the Straits of Gibraltar came into view. It was here that several ships left the convoy, and headed down the west coast of Africa. It was also here that the "tour director", [for want of a better title], came on the air, describing the straits and its history. This officer, whoever he was, made the trip more interesting than it might have been, by pointing out landmarks and places of interest along the whole route, even though some were over the horizon and out of sight. At the end of his little lecture, he announced the ship would be detaching itself from the convoy and would proceed into Gibraltar Harbour in order to drop off a soldier diagnosed with appendicitis. There was a doctor on board but no operating theatre, hence the detour.

The massive natural fortress, universally known as The Rock, was an awesome sight. Pictures in a book were one thing, but actually seeing it up close was something else, and I was amazed to discover how little land there was between the dockside and the place where the face of the rock soared practically vertical into the sky. The *Johann de Witte* edged smoothly into the dock, where the afflicted soldier was carried ashore to a waiting ambulance. Perhaps he was the lucky one. Perhaps after the operation he would spend the remainder of the war on that headland. Half an hour later we cast off, headed out into the Mediterranean Sea and rejoined the convoy.

Next day, after roll call and ship's orders, the following announcement was made — "Because the sea is calm and the forecast for the next few days is good, anyone who wishes to sleep on deck may do so. However, be warned, should the weather deteriorate, all troops must return below deck. Remember no smoking is allowed after sundown." Well, there was one mad rush to reserve your spot. Ernie and I spread ourselves out, staking our claim, while Doug flew down below to get our three blankets, and this is where we stayed for the balance of the voyage. Wally Owen also joined us there.

A hard deck, with one folded blanket as a mattress, and with life jacket and towel for a pillow, is not the most comfortable to sleep on, but it was better than being down below. One can get used to anything when one has to. Fortunately, the weather remained good right into the Indian Ocean, where for a day or two, the ship encountered big swells that made our transport roll and toss around a bit, but most people stuck it out and stayed up on deck.

Sailing through the Mediterranean was quite enjoyable. The deep blue-green sea was calm, and the hot sun shone down from a cloudless sky. We had a pack of cards and a book each to read and swap. Strange how one remembers little details such as the book I had — *The Devil Rides Out*, by Dennis Wheatley. In addition, there was plenty of food to eat, and limewater to drink. At night, the stars sparkled in the clear dense sky, and in daylight, leaping porpoises kept pace with the ship, and flying fish scattered away from the bow. It was a wonderful and fascinating sight!

The slang name of "Limey" for anyone British comes from the fact that for hundreds of years limes and limewater have been used on Royal Navy ships as a preventative measure against scurvy, so that was our main drink. Yet another little gem of useless information.

Our quartet's routine, from that day until the end of the voyage, went something like this. Ablutions, breakfast, roll call and exercises, read for an hour, play cards, [crib], for an hour, eat, drink, take a walk around the deck, then stretch out on our blanket, read for an hour, play cards for an hour and so on and so on. During the afternoon, one or two at a time, we would take off for a shower with our salt-water soap, or try to swap books with someone. Then every second day, we would collect and hold onto our bits and pieces, and just stand there while the deck was swabbed down. Once this had been accomplished, and all was dry once more, down went our blankets, and out came the cards and books again. Oh, the excitement of it all!

Days drifted lazily by, and as we neared Port Said one of those lovely sights that one never forgets appeared. Dotted along the beach, coloured tents had been erected, and with the startlingly white city as a backdrop, it made a stunning picture. At the mouth of the harbour, several ships had been sunk by enemy action, their masts sticking up above the water like so many flagpoles. However, before proceeding through the Suez Canal, the good ship *Johann de Witte* lay at anchor in the inner harbour for two days. For me, it was two eye-opening days.

Nearby was a coal ship, with a couple of barges drawn up alongside. Long, narrow, sloping gangways led from this ship onto the barges, and along these labourers with small baskets of coal on their heads were racing up and down unloading the black cargo. I did not call them labourers; I called them slaves, having never seen people used in such a terrible fashion. How well I remember the feeling of sympathy I felt for these sad, ill-treated human beings, and I was appalled by the whole horrific scene before me. Yet another lesson in my worldly education and perhaps this is where I began to contemplate more seriously the respective merits of colonialism, capitalism, and socialism.

Several times, large manually operated boats, generally referred to as "bum boats", laden with fruit, leather goods, cotton fabrics *etc.* tried to approach the ship in order to sell their wares to the passengers. Each time, loudspeakers came into action warning them to keep away. Time and time again, these small boats ventured nearer and nearer, then beat a hasty retreat as the ship's water hose pipes were blasted onto them.

When eventually we started to move towards and through the Suez Canal, our tour director's voice came over the Tanoy, pointing out the statue of the canal's builder, Ferdinand de Lessop, and the Canal Control Headquarters, with its beautiful blue dome. Alas, the statue is no longer there. The Egyptians pointlessly destroyed it when the canal was taken over and nationalized.

Some miles along the way, our attention was drawn to a huge World War I monument over on the starboard side. This consisted of two separated tall columns, each with the statue of an animal on the outer side. The space between the columns represented the canal and the animals the Turks and the British. The three roads leading up to this edifice represented the three major attacks made by the Turks in that war, in an endeavor to capture this important waterway.

Port Said

Passing by El Cantara, a leave camp for troops stationed in the Middle East, servicemen on the banks shouted remarks, like "When are you going to get your knees brown?" and "What took you so long to get here?" On our return journey, we took revenge for these humorous comments.

Next came Ismalia, then the Large and Little Bitter Lakes, the city of Suez, and onward out into the Red Sea. Now it was hot! The Mediterranean had been hot, but this was like a furnace. A more appropriate name would have been "The Red Hot Sea".

As one can imagine, life aboard ship was monotonous to say the least. Seeing places like Gibraltar and the Suez Canal gave intervals of interest, but once out to sea, it was boring, boring, boring. Now and again, the voice would come on the air with, "We are now passing Jeddah or Mecca or whatever." Being out in the middle of the sea, there was no possible way we could see those cities, but it gave us an idea of where we were.

I cannot remember how many days it took to travel from Port Suez to the passageway between Yemen and Eritrea, but the tedium, coupled with the oppressive heat, was almost overwhelming. Then, after passing through the Gulf of Aden, the *Johann de Witte*, and just one other ship, headed due east along the coast, and out into the Indian Ocean. Over to the north, the Port of Aden came into view, and this was where my old scouting friend, Ned Taylor, was stationed. It looked a terrible place, with barren scorched earth, and hardly a tree in sight.

Next day, as we hit rolling seas, our ship was tossed around as if it was a toy. The strange thing was the big waves did not break, but rose and fell in deep troughs. And there in the middle of this heaving mass of water, appeared a small Arab dhow. At times, it seemed to be perched right on top of the waves, and then it would disappear completely from view. It was an amazing sight! Everyone was watching this balancing act, and I for one was sure the crew would have to be rescued at any minute. Whether it was the design of the boat, or the skillful sailors, I do not know, but the graceful little dhow slowly forged astern and was soon out of sight.

On this, the last leg of our passage to the sub-continent, the four of us speculated as to what the future may have in store. Frankly, because my education had been broadened so much in the last year, I really didn't know what to expect. I would remind the reader that people did not travel so much or so easily as they do today. One's knowledge of a foreign country was gleaned from books or films, and these were mostly biased towards the architectural treasures and more pleasant side of life in those lands. If one emigrated from the UK to Canada, South Africa, or Australia, it was rarely one returned to the home country, even for a visit, unless one had become very wealthy, and could spare the time for the long voyage.

Doug, Ernie and I agreed there would be enormous elephants pulling and pushing massive loads around on the dockside, but once again we were wrong. In fact, it was over a year before I saw my first elephant. The first beast of burden I saw was one I did not expect to see, and that was a camel. I knew there were tigers, baboons, snakes *etc.*, but never expected camels, and the only tiger I saw was in a private zoo.

One day after sighting the dhow, the sea was once again calm and uninteresting, and remained so until early on the 30th day, when word spread like wildfire that land had been sighted. Doug made his way to the bow, but soon came back saying he couldn't see a thing. An hour later though, land and buildings were clearly discernible on the horizon. Closer and closer the buildings came, and now cars could be seen creeping along, what we later discovered was Colaba Beach Road. The air was charged with expectation. There, over to the left was the colossal monument known as the Gateway to India. Then, all at once, our troopship was slowly passing through the dock gates and into one of the inner harbours of Bombay, now Mumbai.

While tugs were pushing and pulling, orders in a strange language were flying between ship and shore. As hawsers were being thrown overboard, there came a slight bump and the *Johann de Witte* had completed its task of delivering 'C' Troop, 270th Anti-tank Regiment to the "Jewel in the Crown". Soon, everyone thought, we will be walking on good old *terra firma* [and the firmer the better], but again we were wrong, for the troops were due to spend two more nights on board ship.

It was Saturday when the ship docked. I say this, because we were allowed off for eight hours the next day, and I'm certain it was a Sunday. After being told to write down the name of the dock [Alexandra I think], and dock gate number, a long lecture followed on how to behave on our first venture into India and this large Indian port.

Down the gangway our inquisitive foursome trotted, through the dock gates, and on into the city. Actually, for the first couple of minutes, it felt quite strange walking on solid ground again. These new arrivals must have stood out like sore thumbs in their serge battle dress, whilst all the servicemen we met were clad in jungle greens, khaki or blue drill uniforms. At a forces canteen, [no NAAFI east of Suez], we obtained a meal and paid for it in sterling, receiving change in rupees and annas. As we contemplated this strange money, a much-tanned soldier approached and recited this little rhyme — "Remember, 16 annas, one rupee; 17 annas, one buckshee." The meal was all right, but it had a quite distinctive taste.

Obtaining a free map, Ernie, Doug, Wally and I ventured out to see as much as possible of this teeming city. On the reverse of the map were directions on how to get back to the docks, so it was obvious that this plan of letting troops off to stretch their legs was a common practice.

Time was short, but we managed to take in the Taj Mahal hotel [then the largest hotel in Asia], the Gateway to India, Queen Victoria's monument, Victoria Railway Station, the Eros Cinema, and the High Court. The main thoroughfares were similar to any large city, and yet different. What made them different was the innumerable bicycles, rickshaws, and horse drawn tongas or gharrys [taxis]. These latter were drawn by tired looking, neglected little ponies.

The main thoroughfares were quite clean and tidy, but down some of the side streets, it was very different, and more like the Orient as I imagined it would be — open-fronted, noisy, smelly shops, selling all sorts of merchandise. There were shoe shops, carpet shops, medicine shops, shops selling car parts, plumbing, beds, clothing, food, and household wares. There were also vendors selling strange looking food being prepared in boiling vats of evil looking oil, and all the while the air was filled with a cacophony of car horns, bells, whistles, and gongs.

However, one of the most unexpected and sordid memories of Bombay was my first encounter with a pimp. This could not have been more than sixteen, and he approached me by saying, "Nice sister, sahib, only ten rupees." With the sheltered life I had led, this was quite a shock. Ernie wanted to know what the youth wanted and when I told him, he said, "Vinnie, don't forget those films we saw back in Conway." I had not, so I didn't need a reminder.

Returning to the ship, everyone was tired and ready for bed. We were just not used to all this walking after being cooped up for over a month.

In the Saturday announcements there were instructions for Monday's collection of rifles and bandoleers, and the timetable for leaving the ship. The troops were ordered to get their kit together after breakfast, and be ready to move by 09:30 hours, but to remain below deck until called.

Before breakfast, however, at around 07:00 hours, word went around that there was some sort of a commotion on deck, and everyone rushed up to see what was going on. On the dockside, surrounded by Indian soldiers with rifles and fixed bayonets at the ready, were assembled two groups of the INA prisoners. At a signal, first one group moved slowly away followed a few minutes later by the other. At the same time, the prisoners started chanting, "Jai Hind, Jai Hind", [leave India, leave India]. It was quite a disturbing scene in a way, because at school we had always been led to believe that people were pleased to belong to this great family known as the British Empire and Commonwealth. I didn't know whether to sympathize with the poor fellows or not. After all, as previously explained, each man was a volunteer.

When they had disappeared from view, and the chanting could be heard no more, it was time to descend below deck for the last time, and await further orders.

The orderly way in which the organization worked was quite impressive. At intervals, companies, platoons, batteries, and troops would be mustered on deck. Then in single file and rough alphabetical order, they would tramp around the ship to the armoury, collect their rifles *etc.*, carry on down the gangway and board the waiting train. As soon as the train had received its full complement of troops, it moved off.

And so our voyage ended. The good ship *Johann de Witte* was left behind, and our journey to the Royal Artillery depot at Deolali began.

Chapter Eight
Deolali

The squalor and filth we saw as the troop-train slowly made its way through some areas of Bombay was indescribable, and as no fences or hedges separated the railway line from the houses, it was easy to witness the abject poverty up close. Charpoys, clay chatties, basins, and other bits and pieces strewn around the back yards, made things look even worse. Some properties appeared to have tomb-like edifices in their back yards, and in one instance, men were actually sitting cross-legged on the flat slab of stone having a friendly chat. I found out later that these may have been Muslim residences, but whether these morbid tomb-like monuments were genuine graves or just replicas, I never did find out. Not all neighborhoods were dilapidated and shabby. Some were a little better than others, but of course the more affluent families would make sure their homes were well away from the railway line.

Upon reaching what I presumed to be the outskirts of the city, I turned to Doug and, with a sigh of relief, exclaimed, "Thank goodness we're out of that lot," but alas, I spoke too soon, because the poverty and slums only got worse. For quite a few miles, the railway line passed through shacks made of bits of corrugated iron, cardboard, and any odd bits and pieces. Not only that, but also hundreds and hundreds of poor half-starved souls lined the track, begging for food or money. Animals in England lived better than this. Slums in Stafford were palaces compared with these places.

Shocked, sickened and horrified is the only way to describe my feelings at seeing these appalling sights, and yet even those words are not strong enough adjectives to express my disgust. How was it possible that human beings had to live under these despicable conditions, and who was responsible for this depredation? Where were the toilets? Where did they cook? How did they earn a living, or did they have to rely on begging? What did they do if someone became ill? Where did they bury or cremate their dead? It was shameful.

Was it the result of the caste system, or was this the fault of the British and Indian governments? Future experience taught me that the governments were partly responsible, but most blame must be assigned to the caste system, which made it virtually impossible for a low caste person to reach a higher level in society. It always puzzled me, how anyone could recognize one caste from another, for they did not all wear identifying marks.

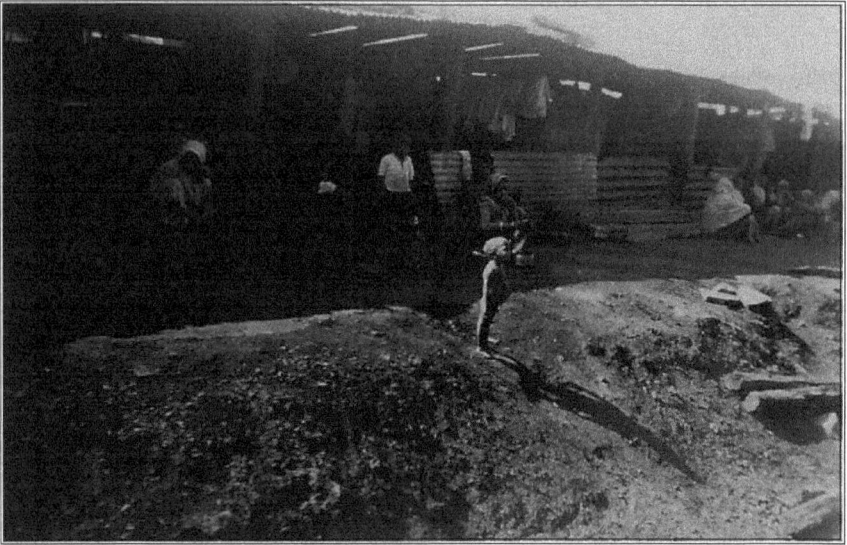

Slums by the Railway

After India gained independence from Britain, the great Mahatma [great soul] Gandhi tried to stamp out this class distinction by living among the untouchables, [the lowest of the castes], in the poorest part of old Delhi, but he never really succeeded. In England, before the war, people would make jokes about this small famous political figure, who would turn up for conferences in simple Indian garb, but the more I read and learned about the man, the more I began to admire him. There is no doubt in my mind that this small, thin, gentle, scantily clad, British trained lawyer with a will of steel, was one of the giants of the 20th century.

Strange as it may seem, however much I try, apart from the ugly side of Bombay, I just cannot remember a great deal about that first journey into India, except that the hard wooden slatted seats were not very comfortable and left a lasting impression where no one could see. The train puffed its way across a narrow plain, and then climbed steeply through hills until reaching a point where it again flattened out onto a more fertile plateau. I seem to remember small farms and villages floating by, and although they were by no means prosperous, they were far better off than those poor hapless creatures we had observed earlier that day.

Although Deolali is only about 120 miles from Bombay, it took roughly four hours to get there. Prior to this rotten war, Deolali, [I have also seen it spelled Devlali], was the main British mental asylum in India, and if one got a touch of the sun or had a mental breakdown, commonly known as the "Deolali tap", this is where one was sent. Back in England, one heard the expression, "so and so has gone Deolali". It meant the same thing. He or she had suffered a nervous breakdown or some other mental disorder. As I was to learn, this and many other every-day sayings and words used in the English language originated here in India, and now here I was, figuratively speaking of course, "going Deolali".

Many months after Japan entered the war, the whole area outside the town, including the hospital, had been converted into a vast transit camp for troops coming in from the UK and elsewhere. Besides the RA depot, there was the Tank Corps, Royal Engineers, Royal Army Medical Corps, and Royal Signal depots. There must have been three or four thousand troops there. About 20 miles further along the railway line there was another large transit camp at a place called Nasik Road.

RASC trucks were waiting at the station to transport the new intake to the camp, where small square barracks made of wood and thatch awaited. I think there were either 8 or 10 soldiers to each billet. Eventually, a Bombardier arrived to take charge of this new intake, and the first thing we did was hand our labeled rifles and bandoleers into the armoury, then it was off to the dining room for a long awaited meal.

Before leaving for the armoury the Bombardier informed one and all that the mattresses [biscuits again], blankets, pillows, and mosquito nets, had been fumigated that very morning, and so should be free of any creepy crawlies. However, at the end of his little chat, the bombardier warned everyone to thoroughly shake out their boots before putting them on in the morning. Exhausted Gunner Gilbert 524 stretched out on the bed, and to his horror, saw several small lizards scampering along the rafters. That night he made doubly sure all his clothing, including boots, were placed inside the mosquito net and the net was well tucked in. He was taking no chances.

Next morning at roll call, an officer described the camp routine and rules. "In two or three weeks' time," he stated, "the battery will be shipping out to

Ranchi, in Bihar State, for jungle training before traveling further east across the Brahmaputra River, into Burma."

The reader may be interested to know that in order to be awarded the Burma Star medal, one had to be stationed east of that massive river for at least forty-eight hours. However, as you will see, fate stepped in with the result that only a few of our draft would qualify for this decoration. Actually, it became quite a thing to boast about, and also a bit of a joke, so it was not unusual to hear a squaddy start a conversation by saying, "Well, of course, when I was east of the Brahmaputra", even if they had never even seen that river. I still sometimes say it.

In the afternoon of that same day, we paraded in our PT kit, and handed in one of our serge battle-dresses in exchange for jungle greens. These consisted of two pairs of trousers, two jacket-like long sleeved tunics, a bush hat, and a monsoon cape. About a hundred yards to the rear of the RA depot office was a row of small shops, where Indian tailors, for a modest price, would make any alterations required. As you can imagine, these people did a roaring trade, but I must admit, they were very good and very fast. On day one I was fitted for uniform No. 1. On day 2 I collected same and left uniform No. 2, which I collected on day 3. What's more, they fitted perfectly. Ten rupees for the lot.

The hot and sticky monsoon season with its tremendous rain storms was drawing to a close, but even so, thick, heavy dark clouds would appear, and, as if someone had taken a knife and sliced them open, a deluge of water would descend and hammer the roof of the basher and pound the earth. Outside of our basher, a truck dumped a large heap of gravel for road repairs, but within a few minutes of the angry clouds opening up, the whole pebbly mound had literally been washed away, the rain was so fierce.

Our regular routine consisted of parades for PT, square bashing, fatigues, swimming and lectures. Amazingly, there were no gun drills. It was easy. There was even a couple of days when parades were cancelled because of inclement weather.

Then, just as we were reconciled to our approaching move east into Burma, and about a week after our arrival, a series of events took place that were to affect my future military career, and in a way, my whole life. It happened like this.

One day a Bombardier stormed into the basher, looked around, then promptly walked over to Ernie and exclaimed, "What the hell are you doing here?" He turned out to be the best friend of Ernie's brother, and was on the permanent staff of the depot. Well, after a long talk that included several bits of useful information, off he went.

100

A few days later, he was back. Seating himself on Doug's charpoy, he said to the three of us, "Listen. There's a notice going up on depot orders [notice board], asking for volunteers, and I have it on a good authority that it's a good number." All three of us laughed at him and replied, "No way are we going to volunteer for anything." You see, there's an old adage in the forces that says, "Never volunteer for anything." He tried in vain to persuade us young gunners to accept this "golden opportunity", but eventually he capitulated, and with a shrug of the shoulders, got up and walked away.

Three or four days later he was back again with, "Look, I don't know where or what it's all about, but I can tell you that I've learned from another source, it's an excellent posting." Once again, we turned him down, whereupon he threw up hands declaring, "Well it's up to you. I've told you what I know, and in any case it can't be any worse than going into the jungle in Burma." And he left it at that.

Doug, Ernie, and I talked it over for a couple of hours and decided, "What have we got to lose?" Our new friend's last sentence about the jungle was, without a shadow of a doubt, the deciding factor. Next day, this brave trio marched into the battery office, where the duty officer asked a few questions, took some notes, then dismissed us. Over the next few days, we attended three interviews where the interrogating officer only seemed to be interested in what we did in "civvy street". Had we been on any committees? Had we participated in any organizations, and had we, in fact done any organizing ourselves? What were our hobbies? What sort of books did we read? What education had we received? Questions on other subjects were presented, but the above were the main ones.

I could truthfully say that I had organized programs and camps for the boy scout troop I had been involved with, but what Ernie and Doug replied to the questions I don't know. Ernie, I felt sure fabricated some of his answers, but Douglas would have answered truthfully. Ernie jokingly told Doug and me that when the officer asked him what his hobby was, he replied, "Women."

Nothing happened. Not a single word did we hear, but towards the end of the third week, the postings were announced, and our names were not on the list. Everyone else was bound for the Jungle Training School at Ranchi. Wally Owen exclaimed to me, "I hope you know what the hell you're doing, because you wouldn't find me volunteering for anything, unless I knew what it was all about. Anyway, the best of luck Vinnie, and do let's try and keep in touch," which we did for many years. Wally was destined to see many more countries than I before eventually ending the war on the island of Cyprus, with the rank of Regimental Sergeant Major.

Another fellow who asked if we could keep in touch was Ron Fox. This was a complete surprise, as this lanky gunner from the east end of London, gave the impression that he couldn't give a damn about anything or anybody, and yet here he was wanting to correspond with me. Sometimes Foxy and I would talk for half an hour or more, about all sorts of subjects, so I knew that under that bluff exterior lay a very different personality from the one he projected. It made me feel quite proud, because he didn't ask the same of anyone else. A rough diamond is the only way to describe Foxy.

It was a bittersweet day when we waved farewell to our friends as they departed for Ranchi. Some of us had been together since Shoeburyness. With shouts of, "Take care of yourselves," and "Keep your head down," we wished them all the best, and they in turn hoped our volunteer jobs would turn out okay. So did we.

The camp seemed dead after their exodus. Our little group of volunteers had grown to five, one of them being Arthur Jones, another fellow from Stoke, but very different from Ernie. We discovered that he had eavesdropped on our conversations with Ernie's bombardier friend, and had quietly volunteered without saying a word to anyone. A self-centred type with a big ego, he was not a popular fellow. The fifth member of the group was a pleasant round faced little chap from Middlesborough.

For a couple of weeks these apprehensive gunners waited around, swimming, performing fatigues, reading, eating, drinking, doing anything to pass the time away. It was a great life. However, when the message arrived to report to the Depot Office, we knew we were on our way. The travel papers indicated we would take such and such a train, and report to GHQ 2nd Echelon, India Command, Jhansi, United Provinces [Punjab]. Doug looked at me, and I looked at Doug, and we both said, almost in unison ,"What the hell is 2nd Echelon, India Command, and where on God's earth is Jhansi?"

Next morning a lorry delivered us to the railway station, where we presented our documents to the RTO. He in turn saw us onto the GIPR, [Great Indian Peninsular Railway] train, and off we started on the three-day, two-night, journey to this mysterious place called Jhansi, and to the even more mysterious GHQ 2nd Echelon, India Command.

Here I was, traveling deep into the heart of Mother India, something I never thought I would be doing in my wildest dreams. Had it only been a few months ago that a trip to Blackpool was the greatest adventure I had experienced? Oh, how my life had changed, and would change even more in the near future. It was then that Doug or Ernie added something like, "And no matter what happens, we stick together, and if possible see India together," which we did, with a few exceptions.

The train compartment was square, with wooden beds that folded down from the walls. The mattress was so thin one could feel every slat. In a recess hidden away in one corner, [it did have a door], was the "toilet". This consisted of two handles to hang on to and two steel footholds, beneath which was a large hole straight on to the railway line. Next morning we learned how lucky we were to have this luxurious convenience.

In a land of this gigantic size, one can travel for hours without seeing anything of interest, then suddenly there may be any number of new intriguing sights, one right after another — temples, towers of silence, water wheels, and structures that looked like small forts. However, one of the most fascinating things I remember is pulling into a station and experiencing the great masses of people and the different sounds and strange smells.

When, during the night our train stopped in a station, it was very eerie indeed. Echoing through the darkness, there came wafting into the carriage muffled cries of "pauni wallah", "char wallah", "dude wallah", and "banjo wallah", only "wallah" sounded more like "walloooo", a sound akin to the cooing of a mourning dove.

As the new day dawned and the sunlight fought its way through the lattice windows, the locomotive came to a complete halt. I scrambled down to find out what was going on, and discovered the train had stopped in an area of small hillocks and scrubland. What happened next was a scene both funny, and beyond belief. The driver gave three long loud blasts on the train whistle, and within seconds a horde of people, some gripping brass containers of water, climbed down off the train and disappeared into the countryside to perform, [we found out later], their morning ablutions. After twenty minutes or so, there were several more powerful whistle blasts — the signal for all the discarded passengers to re-appear and clamber back on board. Following an interval of about five minutes, and a few more rapid "toots, toots" on the whistle, the train resumed its journey to the north.

When one thinks about it, how else were the crammed packed third class passengers going to relieve themselves? Only first class and those compartments reserved for the military had the hole in the floor. At least, that is what I was told. Incidentally, there was no toilet paper provided, but luckily, one of my companions had a paperback book. The title of the book was, *The Devil Rides Out*, the self-same book I read on the good ship *Johann de Witte*. I wonder what comments Dennis Wheatley, [the author], would have made, upon hearing his book had been used for such an essential purpose. I'm sure he would have fully understood that it was all in the service of king and country.

Jhansi Station

Slowly but surely our train made its way north, and when eventually it ground to a halt in Jhansi Station, five stiff, dirty, tired, thirsty and hungry gunners gave a great sigh of relief. We grabbed our gear, stumbled out on to the platform and headed for the establishment that would be our new home for the remainder of our stay in India

Chapter Nine
Jhansi

—————⸺⧓⟩————

I guess it must have been around six o'clock in the evening when our train screeched to a stop in Jhansi station and divested itself of its passengers. We grabbed our gear, stepped out onto one of the longest platforms I had ever seen, [some Havildars reckoned it was the longest in the world], and headed for the RTO. He looked at and stamped our papers, then pointed the way to the exit.

The pick-up truck, which thank goodness, had its tarpaulin removed from the back, was a small old Bedford that had definitely seen better days, and seemed oddly out of place parked as it was, at the end of a line of gharrys. As we walked past these two wheeled carriages, a very distinct and acrid aroma drifted through the air from the poor half-starved emaciated ponies, a smell to which we would quickly become accustomed.

The RASC driver, leaning against the vehicle having a quiet cigarette, looked up as the weary volunteers ambled out of the station. He threw his cigarette to the ground, straightened himself up, brushed some ash from his uniform and called out, "If you lot are bound for GHQ 2nd Echelon India Command, dump your gear and yourselves in the back of the lorry and we'll be off. Do you know if there are any more?"

One of our party replied, "I don't know, but I didn't see any more servicemen, so we must be the lot." So saying, the lads clambered aboard, and with much grinding of gears and a cloud of dust, we shot out of the station yard and headed for our new residence.

As our transport bumped merrily along the sparsely tarmacked route, the driver shouted back tidbits of information as if he was in training to be a tourist guide for Thomas Cook.

"The district we are now passing through is the cantonment," he announced.

"What's the cantonment?" someone asked.

"Oh, it's where the British civilians and many of the senior officers and their families live," he replied. "Over on the left is the garrison theatre, [a grandiose name for a badly neglected cinema], and opposite is the large gym where dances and "housey-housey" is played. [Housey-housey is bingo in civvie street, and the only legally allowed game in the British armed forces where money is involved.]

"Dances!" exclaimed Ernie, suddenly showing interest. "What are they like? Are there many women?"

The driver, after giving a quick backward glance at Ernie, gave a raucous laugh and replied, "They're like a bloody football match. You'll see." The first one we attended proved to us just how right this description was.

"Those buildings you see on the right are the old RASC [Royal Army Service Corps] and REME [Royal Electrical and Mechanical Engineers], workshops. They've been cleaned up and turned into offices." He paused. "That's probably where you people will be working."

GHQ 2nd Echelon Offices

I for one could not quite grasp the significance of this last morsel of information. Here we were, five highly trained anti-tank gunners and yet, if our driver was correct, destined to sit behind a desk. Surely, I thought, there has to be something more sinister behind all this. It just didn't add up.

Suddenly, the tarmac finished as we rolled through a wire fence onto a bare piece of ground and halted outside a long wooden building which housed the camp administrative staff. Our apprentice tour guide dismounted, disappeared inside for a few minutes, then re-appeared with a Sergeant in tow.

"Okay, you lot. Let's have your names." The Sergeant scribbled our names on a clip board and then, pointing in the direction of a line of billets, stated "Find yourselves a bed in basher No. 6, then over to the dining room for a meal. Get a night's sleep, and we will see you here again tomorrow morning at 09:00 hours — any questions?" No one said a word, so after the pause he said, "Till tomorrow morning then," and off he went back into the office.

Billet Group

Basher No. 6 was a long wooden hut with accommodation for about thirty men. Taut long wires, for tying one's mosquito net, ran from one end of the billet to the other, and suspended from the ceiling were three revolving fans equally spaced along the length of the room. Entrances were in the centre and towards each end. The windows, [no glass], were closed off by wooden shutters. There was a shelf over each bed, and a wooden storage box at the foot of the bed. Biscuit mattresses and folded blankets were in place. Arthur wanted to know if they had been fumigated. They had, and our guide added that the billets were sprayed every two weeks. Along the length of both sides, a veranda ran from end to end, and twenty yards from the end of the basher lay the showers and latrines.

Next, after dumping our gear upon a vacant bed, it was off to the cookhouse, where the meal dished up was not bad at all. So far so good, I thought. Perhaps our Deolali Bombardier benefactor had been right after all. Perhaps this was going to be a good posting. Thirst quenched, tummies full, we made our way back to the basher. First thing to do was make one's bed and string up the mosquito net. Second, unpack things like pyjamas, toilet stuff, towel etc. Third, shower, and finally, climb into bed for a much needed night's sleep.

Roman Catholic Church

Next morning, at 09:00 hours, we reported to the Admin Office, and after applying our signatures to the now familiar army forms were instructed to hand in our rifles to the armoury. I have always hated guns, so it gave me great pleasure to carry out this order. Next we were told to proceed along the road to the ex-workshops we had seen the prior evening, and report to Major Herbert in the first dufta to the left. So, along the road we strolled, entered the practically deserted building, and after approaching the only officer on view, came to attention, saluted and introduced ourselves.

"Come in, fellows, come in," said the Major as he looked up from his desk. "Grab yourselves a seat, and I'll try and fill you in as to what goes on here."

When we were all settled, he started with, "I suppose you're all a little apprehensive, so let me put your minds at rest. Sorry to say, and I'm sure you will be pleased to know, you will not be expected to perform any heroic deeds or put your life on the line, but you will be expected to work hard, and the hours, at times, will be long. However, I feel sure, those of you who make the grade will find it most rewarding in more ways than one."

At this point, I was completely mystified, but all became clear as this officer explained over the next half hour or so.

Major Herbert continued, "Up till now, the 14th Army, [popularly known as the "forgotten army"], commanded by General Slim, has been short of men, weapons, material, in fact, everything. So far they have been fighting the Japs with first world war weapons, but that is now changing. Troops and brand new equipment are now beginning to arrive, and will continue to pour into this country in ever increasing numbers. The establishment you will be joining has been set up to keep tabs on all these bodies, organize the movement of same through embarkation ports, transit camps and jungle training schools and when they are battle ready, see them transferred to ALFSEA. If you're the sort of chaps we are looking for, you'll be part of that team."

"GHQ 2nd Echelon, India Command, to put it quite simply, is the army behind the army command known as Allied Land Forces South East Asia [ALFSEA]."

"At first you will be under the supervision of experienced NCOs and officers, and be expected to learn fast. You will work in your appointed departments from 08:00 hours until 12:00 hours. There will then be a break of one hour for tiffin, and from 13:00 hours until 17:00 hours you will tackle a crash course on King's Regulations, army procedures and organization. This routine will last for three months, with only Sundays off, when you will be expected to study. There could be promotion for some of you, but obviously, this depends on how well you perform on the job and in the final examinations."

"However, let me make this absolutely clear, there will be no shirking. This is an important job, and we cannot afford to have any susty wallahs here. If you do not come up to our requirements, you will be immediately returned to a combat unit. Is this perfectly understood by you all?" Obviously, there was more to it than that, but that was the gist of our introductory lecture.

Reaching into a drawer he produced a folder, which he studied for a moment or two, looked up and said, "Beresford?"

Ernie stood to attention and replied, "Sir."

"You, Gunner Beresford, are destined for the casualty section. This office not only covers soldiers who have died, been wounded, murdered, or injured in any way, but also keeps track of any investigations that may possibly be required."

"Gunners Allsop and Gilbert?" Douglas and I stood to attention. "You will be working in what is known as the X1 Section. This office deals with small composite units and groups, sometimes made up of soldiers found unfit for any further active service. Examples would be the permanent staff of railway transport units, military prisons, and jungle warfare schools. Others examples are Army Catering Corps people attached to transit depots or hospitals., REME people attached to artillery batteries — that sort of thing".

I can't remember which offices the others were assigned.

"Any questions?" Silence. Pause... "No? — Okay then, let's go and meet your new colleagues and mentors."

What he failed to mention was that some of these new colleagues would be very resentful towards the new arrivals. These old hands were regular pre-war soldiers, who had spent most of their army career at GHQ India Command, situated in New Delhi. This resentfulness became even more pronounced when some of us were promoted directly up to Sergeant, a rank that had taken them many years, in peace and war, to attain. I could understand their feelings, but we didn't make the rules, and to use a phrase coined in those days, "There was a war on."

Ernie was the first to be dropped off. His dufta was on the opposite side of the road to the ex-workshops, and had been the Admin Office for the previous RASC and REME units. Doug and I were next, and as we entered the office' the eyes of six Havildars, four Sergeants, one Staff Sergeant and a Captain focused upon us. Staff Sergeant Wilson, we soon found out, was the one who really ran the office, because Captain Curzon was as new to this business as we were. Right from the start, the Staff Sergeant let it be known that he was the boss, and showed his distaste and resentment towards these "for the duration of hostilities" soldiers.

Wilson, whose age I guessed was between 35 and 40, had joined the army as a boy soldier, and had spent nearly all his military career in India. He had married an Indian woman, spoke Hindustani like a native, and resided in the cantonment. His wife was undoubtedly the most unattractive and thinnest person I have ever seen in my life. She was so thin that if she turned sideways, no one could see her. I wonder what became of them after India gained independence. They probably stayed there.

Introductions made, Major Herbert left. After a short pep talk from Captain Curzon welcoming us aboard, Wilson took control and introduced us to the other occupants of the office, before handing me over to Sergeant Grubb, and Doug to Sergeant Plastine. The latter was the nicer of the two I thought, because although Grubb was amiable enough he did not go out of his way to impart all the little bits of information that would have made my life somewhat easier.

Sergeants Cartwright, Smith, Plastine, and Grubb

What a change this was from working in a factory. My knowledge of dealing with correspondence and office work was nil, and so when I realized I was only getting 80% help from Grubb, I started to study the existing files on previous problems, apply the same rules, and lay my letters out in a similar fashion.

Within a week, Harry Mason, [another volunteer], Doug, Ernie and I had acquired a bearer named Sam Lal, a small boy about 11 or 12 years of age. Sam would make up our beds for inspection in the morning and remake same by the time we returned from the office. He would take any laundry to the dhobi wallah, make sure it was returned next day, and see that our boots and brasses were polished. His father, who was also a bearer on the camp, kept an eye on him, making sure he did everything correctly. I can't recall how much we paid him, but we all became very fond of Sam, for he was a lovely little round faced lad. It wasn't long before we started to club together to buy him things like shoes and shirts. Some Sundays we would rent cycles, plus one for Sam, and bike along the railway track to the Betwa River for a swim.

Jhansi is a large sprawling city situated on a flat, almost featureless plain, about 120 miles south of Agra. A large fort is situated in the northern part of the city, which for some unknown reason was out of bounds to BORs.

A couple of hundred years ago, a famous battle was fought here between the British and an army led by the Rani of Jhansi. Rather than surrender, this warrior queen rode her horse up onto the ramparts and charged off the highest point, into the besieging forces. For this act she is famous throughout India.

In Sadar Bazaar, the nearest shopping area to the camp, one could purchase almost anything. At one establishment, I ordered two pairs of handmade shoes. My feet were placed on a piece of brown paper and an outline drawn with a pencil. A week later, the shoes were ready and fitted perfectly. In fact, they were probably the most comfortable shoes I have ever owned. Like all the shops, this one was scruffy, and amidst all this untidiness, rubbish and noise, craftsmen sat on their haunches producing the most beautiful leatherwork.

Sadar Bazaar

Of the three places to eat, the best was the Hong Kong Chinese Restaurant, and it became a bit of a ritual that every Friday night a few fellows would eat there, before going to the garrison theatre to see the latest film.

Going to the cinema was sometimes great fun. Whenever the heroine was being lured away by the villain, some bright squaddie would shout, "You'll be sooorrrry," or "Hold on to your knickers lady." Once a film was shown staring Errol Flynn at the head of company of Yankee soldiers, killing hundreds of Japanese and seemingly retaking Burma all on his own. Suddenly the screen was being pelted with bits of junk, coins, ice cream containers *etc.*

accompanied by all sorts of absive remarks. Before there was a full scale riot, the film was stopped and never shown again.

Sadar Bazaar

I should explain,that up to this point in the war, the small 14th Army, under the brilliant leadership of General William Slim, with very little modern equipment and no reinforcements, [this is how it became known as the "forgotten army"], had fought the overwhelming forces of the Japanese Empire all the way back from Malaya, through Burma, finally halting them at the battles for Kohima and Imphal, just inside the Indian border. At one point, Kohima I think, the Japanese were at one end of the tennis courts and the British and Indians were at the other. That was as far as they advanced into India, but it was very precarious at times.

The months and months of monotonous but sometimes interesting office work was broken only by weekends of boredom. If it wasn't for the trips to Agra, New Delhi, Naini Tal, Datia *etc.* and the somewhat zany behaviour of some of the people there, I don't know what we would have done. Perhaps, gone Deolali?

On two occasions I was ordered to attend military funerals. One fellow had died of malaria, and the other poor devil drowned in Jhansi Reservoir. These were very sombre affairs. The funeral party proceeded to the graveside at a slow march, and towards the end of the service, rifle shots were fired as the coffin was lowered into the ground. It was a very sad and distressing couple of hours, and it took a few days, for me at least, to get over it. What a waste of life. Both of them were only nineteen years of age.

Christmas, New Year's Eve, and one's birthday were met with mixed feelings, and thoughts of home. I shall never forget my twenty-first birthday, a milestone in anyone's life. The Admin Office didn't care less what day it was, if your name came up for guard duty, that was it. And so it came to pass that on that momentous night, Gilbert 524 found himself standing behind a barbed wired gate, on a vast plain in the middle of India, rifle in hand, thinking about what it would have been like to celebrate such an occasion with his family and friends back home. A tear spilled down my cheek. I don't think I was cut out to be a soldier. Next night, for the first time in my life, I got a bit tipsy.

Christmas day was always a relaxed time, a time when the rules were bent a little bit. There was always a special dinner, at which an Irish Regimental Sergeant Major, whose job it was to keep discipline at GHQ 2nd Echelon, would try to bring some sort of order. His efforts were rewarded by funny remarks like, "Get stuffed," or "Up the inniskillings," or "You know where you can stuff your yellow heckle" [or words in that vein].

Of course, the Chaplain would always make an appearance and make a short speech. One year he started out by saying, "As you all know, today is the day when Jesus Christ was born." Immediately, my comedian buddy, Sergeant Ernest Beresford started singing, "Happy birthday to you, happy birthday to you," and within a few seconds, the whole mess was joining in the chorus. Our Inniskilling Fusilier friend was not amused, but the Reverend howled with laughter.

Actually, I felt the Chaplain quite enjoyed himself, because after he had said grace, he walked around the tables, making chitchat. He had a special word with Ernie, which must have been some kind of joke, because Ernie and the fellows sitting nearby suddenly roared with laughter. The joke, about the three wise men, was relayed around, but for the life of me, I cannot recall it. That little funny did more for the chaplain's popularity than all his sermons put together.

The CO and the 2nd in command would also join us for a short time, and before taking his leave, he would perform the customary duty of wishing everyone a happy Christmas and New Year. Then, raising his glass, he bade the whole mess to rise and makes the loyal toast to the king, followed by the singing of the national anthem.

The Sergeant's Mess was a long wooden building, containing a bar at one end and kitchens and dining room at the other. Adjacent to the bar was a space about 30 feet square, furnished with a few armchairs and small low tables.

Sergeant Gilbert, Christmas 1944

The remaining space was resplendent with dining tables that accommodated four, six, or eight people. On the outside, suspended by wires were numerous large tin cans, into the bottom of which was placed a great dollop of jam, plentifully laced with DDT. The idea was that the jam attracted the flies and mosquitoes and the DDT would kill them off.

For some reason, one had to take one's hat off before entering the mess, not after entering. Anyone disregarding this rule could be fined, the money going into the mess funds. There was also a monthly mess fee of 25 rupees. This money paid for the bearers who waited tables, improvement of the facilities, purchase of recreational equipment, and little extras to add to the menu.

Photographic Shop, Sadar Bazaar

One slice of luck we found at Jhansi was that once a month we could buy one roll of film from a photographic shop in Sadar Bazaar. Actually, it was RAF film that had been deemed redundant for some reason. We gathered that it was very wide film for use in reconnaissance flights, and someone had the bright idea to cut the film into usable rolls for small hand held cameras. I immediately wrote home asking mother to send a Kodak Brownie box camera she had. This arrived about three months later packed in a biscuit tin. As one can see from the photographs, they are very grainy, and a few have a shaft of light down one side. Poor they may be, but it is a record of the things and places I experienced.

Chapter Ten
The Dance

———⎯⎯⎯⎯⎯———

The dances, you will recall, were described by our apprentice tour guide, [the truck driver who picked us up at Jhansi railway station], as being like a football, [soccer] match, and that pretty well hits the nail on the head, or more appropriately, the ball in the back of the net. The struggle that lower rank soldiers had in order to obtain entrance into the large "ballroom", [actually the camp gymnasium], was something to behold, with everyone pushing and shoving.

It goes without saying that officers and their wives or partners were allowed to enter in a more civilized manner through a less congested door. So were the small number of Anglo-Indian women, a few Indian ladies, and our very own four British ATS [Auxiliary Territorial Services] girls.

The officers, ATS girls and some BORs wore smart khaki drill uniforms, while a third of the men were dressed in jungle greens. All officers' partners, plus the Anglo-Indian ladies, were attired in variously light coloured, long sleeved dresses, while only a couple of the Indian ladies wore sari's. Dainty little Sergeant Mary Grace Gidla from my office did not attend any of these functions. Who knows, perhaps her lawyer father disapproved of his daughter mixing with these rough military men.

Once inside, it became patently clear that the soldiers outnumbered the women by at least five or six to one. So you may ask, as I asked myself, how on earth did any of these brave ballroom gladiators manage to get a whirl around the floor? The answer is as follows.

Try to imagine the scene. The giant gymnasium charmingly decorated with climbing bars up the side walls, to which the climbing ropes were exquisitely looped and tied. The gym mats were beautifully stacked in one corner and the vaulting horses corralled in another. Inhabiting the stage was a small five or six piece band, and there, sitting to one side was our dear "friend" from the Inniskilling Fusiliers, the very daunting Discipline Regimental Sergeant Major for the camp. On the other side of the stage, sat four hefty looking Redcaps [military policemen].

About ten minutes after the last combatant was allowed to squeeze in through the door, the RSM, who would act as referee for the night, stood up, approached the microphone, gave it a couple of taps, and called for order. After the hall had quietened down, he began by saying, "We're all here tonight to enjoy ourselves, and if you all obey the rules, I'm sure everyone will have a pleasant time." So saying, he then read out the rules for the evening:

[1] Every other dance will be an "excuse me" dance, whether it be a waltz, fox trot, tango, whatever.

[2] Only when the whistle is blown can one break up a couple with a polite "excuse me". [He repeated this three times.]

[3] There will be no brawling, and if a couple is assailed by two or more at the same time, which frequently happens, it is the lady's prerogative as to whom she dances with. [This, he also repeated three times.]

[4] All troops are instructed to be on their very best behaviour; otherwise, they will be evicted and placed on a charge.

So there we were, approximately two to three hundred officers and other ranks, and about forty or fifty women. The RSM's voice continued to ring out, declaring to all present that the first dance of the evening would be a slow fox trot, at the same time making it absolutely clear it was not an "excuse me" dance.

The next dance was an "excuse me" quickstep, and again came a warning to wait for the whistle, which blasted out about every three or four minutes. So you see the truck driver had been correct. It was like a football match, but without the linesmen. Another description would be the start of a hundred yards sprint, for one could see the fellows getting ready to race on to the floor, [or should that read "battlefield"], in order to try and claim a dance.

This pattern was followed all night long, when, as the next "excuse me" dance was announced, or as soon as the whistle blew, there was one almighty sprint on to the dance floor to lay claim to a partner. The women and girls must have been worn out by the time the evening came to a close, having had to dance with some fellows who were definitely not in the Fred Astaire class. Some fellows ambled around like baby elephants, others just shuffled around the floor, and all of them just wanting the chance to hold a girl in their arms for a few minutes. Sad, really. Obviously the female martyrs quickly discovered who were the good dancers and who were not, and who smelled sweetly, and who were drenched with perspiration, for despite the doors and windows being left open, and the fans working overtime, the heat generated by all these steaming bodies became almost unbearable. It was like dancing in a sauna bath

Enter one Gunner Ernest Beresford [he hadn't received promotion yet], who was soon participating in every dance, and not just the "excuse me" ones. One officer, no doubt on orders from his better half, walked over and asked him if he would like to partner his wife in the next dance. Other women just walked across and invited him to be their next partner. As I have already related, my friend was not only a beautiful ballroom dancer, but he had all the chat and a mischievous smile to go with it.

I have no doubt at all, that it had been "suggested" by the CO that officers and their wives should attend these dances as a moral booster. I also have no doubt that the chaperoned single Indian and Anglo-Indian girls came in the hopes of finding a husband.

This farcical, yet greatly entertaining evening ended with everyone standing to attention while the little band played a squeaky rendition of God Save the King, an anthem most of the ladies present were more than glad to hear. I looked up the meaning of "rendition" in the dictionary and it was, "The execution of a dramatic or musical composition." Sorry to say, the little band certainly did murder some of the tunes that night.

The band began to pack up their instruments, the lads drifted back to their bashers, and the brave females were escorted back to their homes or billets, where they could plunge their poor bruised aching feet into bowls of hot water laced with copious amounts of epsom salts.

If I may parody one of Winston Churchill's most famous phrases, "Never on the dance floor, was so much owed by so many, to so few."

119

Chapter Eleven
Datia

It was all a big fiddle really. All the names of servicemen on the establishment were, supposedly, placed in a hat and the names drawn would be the lucky people who would take this most interesting of trips. We must have been at GHQ 2ⁿᵈ echelon, for about a year, when Doug's name came up, and when our "beloved" Staff Sergeant Wilson inquired, "Who would you like to go with?" he replied, "Sergeant Gilbert." So that was how we came to travel together, and why I say, it was all a big fiddle.

Datia, at that point in India's history, was a small princely state about two hours' drive away, and as we had learned from previous visitors, it was an experience not to be missed. Each week, the Maharajah of Datia invited eight or ten servicemen to be his guest for three days, although we, and as far as I know no one else, had ever met him.

At the unearthly hour of 06:00, our little group could be seen climbing aboard a lorry and heading out to the north west. We sat on wooden benches fitted along the inside of the lorry, and the continuous bouncing up and down did not make for the most comfortable of rides. It was impossible to turn the other cheek, because both cheeks were being equally battered. At our feet, the large packs containing our personal gear had to retrieved repeatedly, as they were tossed around all over the floor.

Across the Miadam, through poor miserable villages, our conveyance made its way, until the driver shouted something that only the squaddies near him could hear. They stood up, so we stood up also, and looking straight ahead was a sight that could only have come right out of a Hollywood film.

As the massive stone walls of this small city came nearer and nearer, the setting became more and more fantastic. Sentries, clad in bright blue uniforms stood at the gates, and, believe it or not, were armed with spears. I fully expected Errol Flynn, Cary Grant, Victor McClagen, or even Sabu, [film stars of yesteryear], to appear at any moment. It was unreal.

Datia City Gate

The lorry slowed down to a snail's pace as it passed through the gates, and then crept through the crowded narrow streets and bazaars. The smell from the street food vendors and open drains was beyond words. These open sewers were small trenches running along each side of the street, so the only way one could gain access to the "shops" was by crossing a small footbridge.

At the entrance to some of these shops, sat basket ware cribs holding small babies, only some of whom were covered with a cloth or mosquito net. Those tots not protected by a net had flies crawling all over their little bodies and faces. It was disgusting. The mother or father would occasionally waft a fan or hand across the child scattering the flies, but the pests were soon back. Is it any wonder that disease killed so many of these people?

Suddenly, we were outside the city walls again, but the strange thing was, there was no guard on this side of the city. A few minutes later the lorry came to a halt outside a moderately large white one story building. This was the guest house, our resting place for the next three days. A small middle-aged man in a wrinkled off-white linen suit and pith helmet welcomed the party, ending with the announcement that refreshments would be served in the dining room immediately everyone had freshened up.

It was like having another breakfast, for the ample refreshments consisted of bacon, eggs, toast, tea etc. While the lads were filling their stomachs, the little man explained that he was the state's Minister of Education and presented our program for the next three days. Starting straight after tiffin, and following a visit to the local prison, there would be a tour of the country palace. Tomorrow would be a free day to do as we wished, and on our departing day, we would inspect a new housing project.

The Maharajah, a Muslim, had two palaces and two harems, one in the city, and one here in the countryside, the latter palace being situated at the head of a small, shallow, foul looking elongated "lake". Our accommodation lay about one hundred yards away from the palace, looking out onto the side of this scruffy weed ridden bit of water. It all looks very nice in a photograph, but photos can be misleading.

We were billeted two to a room, and Doug and I, being the only sergeants present, were allocated the nicest room. It was nothing elaborate; in fact, it was quite bare and plain. The beds, complete with mosquito nets, were comfortable and the sheets crisp and white. There was also a bearer for each room.

Palace Guest House

Before embarking on this trip, Doug and I talked to several fellows who had been there previously, and we discovered that a few miles away was a hill covered with over sixty Jain temples. Alas, one could only get there by gharry, [a two wheeled, pony drawn vehicle, with seating for two looking forward, and two passengers looking to the rear] along a rough track across the Miadam. Doug and I knew we just had to try and see this place. Consequently, before setting out for the prison we got hold of our bearer, and with promises of many baksheesh for him and the driver, managed to persuade him to hire a gharry, organize some food and drink, and guide us to this sacred spot.

Country Palace

Now back to the first day at Datia, and our visit to the prison.

Charles Dickens and Rudyard Kipling would have been in their element describing this unbelievable place of incarceration, for it resembled something from Victorian times, or even before. When we entered, a few raggedly clothed inmates were spreading what looked like clean straw or rushes over the entrance floor. My feelings are hard to describe, for it was as if one could feel and sense the cruelty that took place in this horrible institution. What sickened me most of all were two particularly inhuman and disgusting scenes. One was the incredible sight of a treadmill and men actually working it, and the other was seeing poor wretches with balls and chains attached to their legs. Never in my wildest dreams did I ever envisage seeing anything like this. It was like stepping back into the dark ages.

I breathed a sigh of relief when we departed that horrific place and stepped out into the bright clean sunlight again. Everyone was strangely quiet as we climbed aboard the rickety bus, but then the lads started to make remarks like, "Poor sods," and "Surely it can't be right to treat people like that, even if they are criminals?" I just cannot find the words to describe my sympathy for these ill-used wretched human beings. It was awful.

Our party gradually wended its way towards the country palace, an edifice that was a bit of a disappointment. What I expected I don't know, but this was not my idea of a palace, for the furniture was poor and the rooms run down and shabby. Even the driveway was pot-holed and greatly in need of repair.

The one room that does stick in my mind was about fifteen feet square and lined with rows and rows of deep shelves. From these shelves, the unseeing eyes of nearly two hundred tigers stared vacantly out at the visitors. It seems the maharajah enjoyed hunting and shooting these wild animals, which he subsequently had skinned. The skins were then rolled up in such a manner that the heads faced into the room. How individuals can find enjoyment in the killing these beautiful creatures, or any wild animal, is beyond me.

Unfortunately, we were not allowed anywhere near the harem, but we were allowed to visit the private zoo, which again was not very impressive. It was here that I saw an elephant and a tiger for the first time since arriving in India. Jumbo was a giant of a thing, and I marvelled at the way in which his small keeper handled him.

Sergeant Allsop, Bearer, and Sergeant Gilbert

Back at the guest house, just as we were leaving our room for dinner, our bearer met us with the news that all arrangements had been made for tomorrow's adventure and that we would be leaving directly after breakfast.

Dinner that night, and the following night, consisted of a mysterious looking stew that was laced with a fair amount of curry, so much so, that the first mouthful had all the diners gasping for breath. Luckily, there was plenty of cold water handy to ease our burning throats. Also on the table was lots of butter and small pieces of bread that I can only describe as being like French stick. Desert was a mixture of fruit, with loads of custard, followed by copious amounts of char.

Next morning, Doug and I climbed aboard the waiting gharry, so the bearer sat up-front beside our chauffeur for the day. It took more than an hour to reach the hill, over a barren and arid terrain. A few times, small herds of goat could be seen, munching away at poor measly thorny bushes that dotted the landscape. No one appeared to be looking after them, so we wondered if they were wild, but our bearer replied, "Kutchnay sahib."

Because of the poor condition of the track, the speed of the gharry varied from a trot to slow, but eventually we arrived at our destination.

The Jain religion, founded by Mahavira, is much older than Christianity, dating back to 600 BC and preaches non-violence and vegetarianism. Jains are a sect of the Hindu religion, similar, I suppose, to the way Protestants and Catholics are branches of Christianity.

Jain Temples

The scene before us was something to behold, especially when our bearer informed us there was one temple for Mahavira, and one for each of his sons and daughters. There were sixty two temples all told, so Mr. Mahavira must have spent a very busy life.

Some of the temples were small, others were dilapidated and needed maintenance, but never the less, it was quite a remarkable and impressive sight. Obviously the largest one was dedicated to Mahavira himself, while the others varied in size according to the importance of the individual.

Scanning the view from the top of the knoll, it was as if the whole landscape had been deserted. Apart from the bearer and gharry driver, we appeared to be the only human beings on this earth, and it gave one a very peculiar and eerie feeling. The air and atmosphere was so quiet and ubiquitously still, my friend and I could have been on the moon.

After we explored the site, lunch appeared. I have an idea it was chapatis with some sort of spicy filling, washed down with tepid char. Not very appetizing, but we were two hungry young men.

Before climbing aboard our chariot for the return journey, Doug and I meandered around the mound one more time, taking photographs of this revered place. As Doug quite rightly remarked, "This is a day we will remember for the rest of our lives."

I think I replied something like, "You're wrong, Doug. These whole three days will be remembered for the rest of our lives."

The poor little pony received a tap on its skinny rear end, the gharry moved forward, and we set off along the rough and dusty track. As we retreated, I found it difficult to pull my eyes away from this sacred hill with its multitude of temples, but gradually it disappeared from view.

Next morning the Minister of Education arrived with his little bus, to show us the Maharajah's new housing project. The minister explained that the prince was trying to get rid of slums in the city by moving families to this new housing estate outside the city walls. As he finished his speech, the bus came to a halt opposite rows of stark, square concrete dwellings, [boxes], which he invited the group to inspect.

He took the group to one particular house that was kept as an example for the inhabitants to copy. The small "bathroom" had a concrete table along one wall, on which stood a wash basin and a couple of chattis. The toilet was a large bucket with a seat, and this night soil needed to be emptied each day. The remaining rooms, two bedrooms, living/dining room, and kitchen, were equally as utiliterian. The cooking fireplace was made of concrete or some sort of brick, and this was vented out through the wall. Each house had a small strip of land, front and rear, so they could keep a goat or some other animal.

The snag was, our minister informed us, the people moved into these new premises had to be educated in the use of each room, and continually monitored in what they did where.

"Each week, for two months", he told the group, "I, or my assistant, must visit each newly installed family, to ensure everything is being done correctly. There is then be a gap of two or three weeks, when the family goes unsupervised. Very often, upon our return we find a goat in the bathroom, cow dung fuel stacked in the living room, and so on. My assistant and I then have to start all over again instructing these people upon the hygienic way to live."

What I could not understand was, they had electric light, so why couldn't they have had small electric stoves? I asked the question, but did not receive a satisfactory answer. I think money was one of the problems, but how much extra would it have cost? Surely, in the long run, it would have been much cleaner and healthier than burning wood or cow dung.

It was quite a common sight to see large areas adjacent to villages or houses covered with what looked like curved dinner plates with one section of the rim cut flat. Standing up on edge, these plates are made from cow dung, which the women collect and pat with their hands into shape. The dung is then set out in the sun to bake. I just hope the women washed their hands before starting to make chappatis, especially the ones we ate at the Jain temples.

The tour over, the little bus conveyed the group back to the guest house where sandwiches and char awaited. This was followed by a short farewell speech thanking us for coming and taking such an interest in the developments going on there. After he had finished, the lads turned their eyes towards Doug and I, so I gingerly rose to my feet and thanked the minister for a most enjoyable and enlightening three days. I also asked the minister to pass on to the Maharajah our appreciation of the hospitality extended to the group. Well, my few words went something like that, for to tell the truth I had never been called upon to make a speech like that before. Doug said it sounded okay, so I guess it was.

We collected our gear, and with handshakes and thanks all round, we clambered aboard the waiting lorry. Back through the city walls and congested streets we travelled, until we were out on the miadam once again. It was late afternoon when our driver returned his passengers safe, but not too sound, to GHQ 2nd Echelon, India Command, and back to the 20th century.

Another chapter in my worldly education.

Chapter Twelve
All Creatures Great, and Small, and Nasty

Of all the things I dreaded in India, the creepy crawly insects were the ones feared most, especially after my encounter with a battalion of what were commonly known as stink bugs.

It happened this way.

One morning, after an extremely restless night, I got out of bed to find parts of my body, face and head covered with red blotches. Immediately I thought the worst. All the lads steered clear of me, so I just knew I had caught some horrible tropical disease that would unquestionably transport me from this earthly world to the next, or leave me terribly disfigured for life. Needless to say, I hurriedly made my way over to the sick bay.

Afflicted as I was, I felt sure I would be taken directly into the MO [Medical Officer], but instead the Corporal Medic took a quick glance at my forehead and in my hair, and calmly told me, "Sit over there, Sergeant."

After what seemed an eternity, I was ushered into the doctor's office, where once again my head and body, including the nether regions were inspected. As the MO moved from one part of my manly frame to another, the silence was interrupted with lots of "mmms" and "ahs". It spoke well of the British Army that they employed officers with such an expansive vocabulary.

"Okay," he said finally, "Put your clothes back on, and the Corporal will go over to the billet with you and take care of things." Raising his voice he called the Corporal into his office and ordered, "Go back to the basher with the Sergeant and have a look at his bed. If it's what we suspect, you had better take a can of petrol with you."

Not only did he bring a can of petrol, but also one of those long old fashioned bayonets. On the walk over I questioned the medic, but all he would say is, "Just wait and see." Anyway, by the time we arrived back at the basher, Sam Lal, my bearer, had made up my bed ready for the daily inspection, so you can imagine my surprise when the Corporal grabbed hold of my mattress, pillow, blankets and sheets and threw them outside on the verandah.

Back inside the basher, he invited me to "Look at this." So saying he forced the bayonet under the ropes of the charpoy, [bed], and eased them out of the way, revealing dozens of small red insects, about the size of lady bugs. He then proceeded to cut through the ropes on other parts of the bed showing hoards more of these nasty little devils. I was visibly shaken. No wonder my night had been so restless.

"Get your pyjamas, take them outside, shake them well and spread them out on the verandah," he ordered. This done, I watched him spray them with DDT. "Leave them there for a few hours, and then send them to the dhobi wallah, [laundry], tonight."

"Whatever you do," he emphasized, "do not squash any of these critters, because the smell will be awful. I don't know the correct name for them, but in the sick bay we call them stink bugs." I didn't want to get near the damn things, never mind squash them.

Next we gently let down the sides of the mosquito net and, looking into the corners, what did we see but loads more crawling over one another like bees in a hive. We untied the net from the ceiling wire, letting it drop carefully and slowly onto the wood and sisal charpoy. Next the charpoy was taken outside, the blankets etc. placed on top, and the whole assembly carried about a hundred yards away from the buildings. He then doused everything with petrol and set the whole lot on fire. A minute later I raced back to the basher, grabbed my sleeping togs off the verandah, flew back, and tossed them onto the funeral pyre. Gilbert 524 was not taking any chances. Just to be on the safe side, I borrowed the DDT spray and drenched the inside of my storage box and all around my bed area with the insecticide.

After the cremation, the corporal and I wandered over to the QM's store. The Corporal filled in several forms, and across the counter came a new pillow and blankets, which I immediately shook out much to the amusement of the issuer. "They're all right," he said, "Everything gets fumigated every two weeks."

The next thing he asked was, "What sort of a charpoy do you want?"

I didn't know you could choose, so I replied, "What sort have you got?"

With a flip of his hand and a nod of the head, he invited me into the bowels of the store, where about twenty wood and rope charpoys and a few steel ones were stacked. Without hesitation I stated emphatically that I would take a steel one. There were no springs on the bed, just flat criss-crossed metal straps, but that didn't worry me as long as there was no place for those little red vermin to make their home.

And so, with the help of one of the store keepers, we trundled back to the basher with my new charpoy, plus mattress, blankets, pillow and mosquito net. As luck would have it, because it was June and boiling hot, my Canadian army blanket had been placed in my storage box, while the other two had been laid between the bottom bed sheet and the mattress. I would have been quite upset if that blanket had gone up in smoke. I'd had it a long time, and as I previously mentioned, I still have it today.

Mission accomplished, it was back to the sick bay, where layers of slimey ointment was applied to my poor disfigured torso and head. The medication smelled absolutely putrid, so much so, that when I joined Ernie and the lads for tiffin, they all held their noses and pulled away from me asking, "Have you had an accident in your trousers?" or words to that effect.

Again, on walking into the office that afternoon, Staff Sergeant Wilson took one look at me, sniffed the air, and being an old hand knew exactly what my problem was. He reluctantly let me have the afternoon off, which I utilized by visiting Sadar Bazaar to purchase some new sheets, pillow cases and pyjamas. You see, the army does not provide these little extras.

After a couple of weeks or so of this greasy fragrant treatment, the blotches faded and finally disappeared, but from then on, I examined my mosquito net and bed linen much more frequently — and so did my friends.

Then there was the evening when a few of us gathered together as usual to chat and share a mug of Syed Wazir Ali's horrible char. On these occasions we would share seating on our storage boxes and charpoys, and on this particular night, everyone was nattering away when one of the fellows suddenly jumped up on a box, pointing at something about six feet away. That something was a spider about the size of a large saucer, scurrying hither and thither all over the floor.

Like the fearless, highly trained soldiers that we were, we instinctively took evasive action. Up onto a box I jumped, while others picked up their feet up onto a charpoy. This spider then became the target for anything that was at hand — boots, small packs, ammunition pouches *etc*. After it was declared dead, all the lads inspected it before it was finally kicked out onto the piece of land separating the bashers. The repulsive thing had a large head, from the top of which protruded two fierce looking antlers.

Last of all let me tell you about the time I had to visit the toilet in the middle of the night. Practically everyone owned a battery operated torch, because the roadway from the duftas to the bashers was not lit up, and inside the camp perimeter lighting was extremely poor, and so on this particular night I was especially glad I possessed one.

The call of nature came around 02:00 hours, so I struggled out of the mosquito net, reached for my flashlight, and toddled off to the latrine. The lower four feet of these buildings were brick and concrete, which was topped by a wooden partition up to the sloping roof. This left a small shelf where the wooden construction met with the concrete wall. Penetrating the darkness with my torch, and with a great sigh of relief, I lowered myself upon the throne. Sitting there quite contentedly, I probed the darkness once again and discovered to my horror that a few inches away from my head was a dirty great scorpion lounging on the shelf. Believe me, that was the quickest visit to the washroom I have ever made. It was certainly no time for arsing about.

So there you have it — bugs, spiders, and scorpions.

There were also monkeys, camels, water buffalo, kite hawks, vultures and other creatures, but they were nothing compared with the smaller wildlife described above.

And all for king and country.

Chapter Thirteen
Agra

This famous city lies about 120 miles to the north of Jhansi, and when Doug, Ernie and I realized how near it was, it only became a matter of time before we made our way there. The great attraction, of course, was the Taj Mahal. Bala Singh insisted the best time to see this famous mausoleum was when the moon was full, but unfortunately, we were never able to arrange this.

Unfortunately, when the leave opportunities did come along, our trio, because of the duty roster, were unable to make the trip together. On the first visit, Sandy Harris was my companion, while on the second occasion it was Steve Taylor.

Sandy and I managed to get a ninety-six hour pass, which meant we could travel up one day, see the Taj the next day, visit the Red Fort on the third day, and return to Jhansi on the fourth. As you can imagine, we were both quite excited at taking our first excursion on the sub-continent and laid out our plans accordingly.

It was not, however, a ninety-six hour pass in the true meaning, but was another bit of a fiddle. GHQ 2nd Echelon India Command was a non-combat unit, so as long as someone was on duty, in case of an emergency, we could within reason, do whatever we liked on Saturdays and Sundays. Therefore, the wangle was to apply for a forty eight hour pass and add this on to the weekend. The Admin Major knew what was going on, but like Nelson, turned a blind eye to the practice.

The train journey was quite uneventful except for the imposing sight of the great fort high on a plateau overlooking the city of Gwalior. The Maharajah of Gwalior was a very powerful man at that time, ruling one of the largest princely states in India.

On the outskirts of this city, a Parsee Tower of Silence came into view, with its ever-present flock of vultures and kite hawks hovering and whirling overhead, no doubt looking forward to their next feast. The only other one I had seen was near Deolali. The Parsee religion was founded in about 600 BC, and its followers worship the earth and all the elements, so they cannot bury their dead in the ground or at sea, nor can they cremate the body. This problem is resolved by laying the corpse on a huge stone slab, like an alter I suppose, in the Tower of Silence, where they are left to the care of the vultures etc.

Bala Singh told me a flame is always kept burning in the tower, and in some cases, the bodies are chopped up before the birds feast on them, but I have never been able to verify this. What happens to the bones after they have been picked clean I do not know, but obviously, there must be some sort of a spiritual ceremony. It may sound gruesome, but is it any worse than other ways of disposing of the dead?

When we eventually arrived at Agra, it felt as if half the population of India had crowded into the station. It was a battle just to get off the train, never mind the platform. This was no place for good manners, with people pushing, shoving, and ramming their way through the mob using bits of luggage as battering rams. Not only that, but the noise was unbelievable. At last, carried along by this human tide, Sandy and I broke out of the building, made our way to the taxi rank, and about thirty minutes later arrived at the Armed Forces Rest Centre.

After registering and dumping our gear on the allotted beds, we made our way to the canteen for some much needed food and drink. I do not think we did anything for the rest of the day, except explore the facilities, go for a swim, lounge around by the pool and partake of liquid refreshment. It was a hard life, but someone had to do it.

Next morning, after a hearty breakfast, we took a gharry to see the Taj Mahal. The driver explained that, for a few extra baksheesh he would make a detour so we could see this jewel from a special vantage point, which he assured us, "Will make you a very happy, sahib." Sandy, after getting my agreement told the driver, "Teek hi," and away we went.

There was quite a lot of traffic on the road in places, and I was beginning to think we were never going to get there, when suddenly, after making a sharp left hand turn, followed by a few more twists and bends, the gharry pulled to the side of the road and came to a halt. As Sandy and I were in the backward looking seats, we just sat there for a couple of moments, until the driver called back, "Shufti sahib, decko sahib decko," and there, following the outstretched arm and pointing finger, was one of the most stunning sights I have ever seen.

The Taj Mahal

A few hundred yards away stood this most perfect of buildings, all white and shimmering in the haze of the blazing sun. It was truly unbelievable. The whole enormous mass of marble appeared to glow, as if it had a halo around it. I read somewhere a description of it as a "poem in marble", and I guess that says it all.

I cannot describe my feelings at that particular moment because they are lost in time. I just remember gazing in absolute wonder. Sandy gasped and exclaimed something like, "Bloody hell!" It was that incredible. More educated men than me have written about this edifice, and none, I feel, have done it the justice it deserves. How can one describe something so perfect? It's one of those things a person must see in order to believe.

In those days of the British empire, the whole approach to the Taj Mahal was completely vacant, and our vantage point offered an uninterrupted vista. Alas, factories and other structures have been built in the area, and damage from pollution is causing great concern. I'm glad I saw it before these sacrilegious acts took place.

If we had approached along one of the two main roads, we would have been deprived of this special view, so Sandy and I were more than pleased to hand over a few extra rupees. The rise in the ground where the gharry pulled to a stop could not have been more than fifteen or twenty feet, but it was enough to allow this unusual, about forty-five degrees to the gateway, glimpse over the surrounding wall.

The Taj Mahal

Another few minutes and the gharry dropped its two teenage passengers outside the huge elaborate gateway. Awe struck, we walked through the entrance to be presented with the picture everyone has seen in so many magazines, books, and travel films. It was magnificent! Never in my short life of nineteen years did I ever believe I would actually see this wonder of the world.

The black cypress trees, reflected in the central pools, were in great contrast to the huge white tomb, and as we slowly made our way towards it, the immensity of the building became more and more astounding. The platform alone must be at least fifteen feet high. Before climbing the broad marble stairway to this raised area, shoes must be removed. A couple of rupees to the shoe guard ensured, we hoped, our footwear would still be there when we returned. When viewed from the gateway this stairway is completely out of sight, sort of melting into the marble dais.

Across the platform we strolled, ascended a few more steps, and came face to face with the huge archway into the inner chamber. All around, there were passages of the Koran, black marble embedded in the white, and garlands of flowers, the petals of which were made of several different coloured stones. In the centre of the inner chamber, stood two replicas of the real tombs located in a chamber twenty feet below. These were also ornately and beautifully decorated with holy words and multi coloured flowers. Incidentally, the real tombs down below were also open to the public. Why the replicas? I do not know.

Surrounding the real tomb is the most remarkable marble screen. I may be wrong, but I think it was carved from one piece of stone. Octagonal in shape, it measures about twenty to thirty feet from one flat side to the other. The workmanship is exquisite. Is it any wonder it took twenty years to complete?

After walking across the platform to look out over the River Jumna, we climbed the right rear minar to obtain yet another very different view of this masterpiece. Years later, I discovered that these minars had been erected so that they leaned slightly away from the Taj Mahal. The theory was that, should there be an earthquake, they would fall away from the main edifice.

In order to keep the religious and political peace, Shah Jehan first married a Moslim lady, then a Hindu lady, until eventually he became the proud possessor of thirty-one wives, and I'm sure everyone knows, this remarkable monument to love was built for Mumtaz Mahal, his favourite wife. I understand that it was his intention to build, for himself, an exact replica on the other side of the river, only this time in black marble. Unfortunately, his son usurped the throne and imprisoned him in the red fort, but just try to imagine what an incredible sight that would have been.

The two buildings standing away on either side of the Taj Mahal are also to placate religious factions. Although they appear somewhat similar, one is actually a Mosque and the other a Temple, and these too were elaborately decorated.

And so, after about two or three hours at this magnificent showpiece and gardens, Sandy and I took our leave, clambered aboard a gharry and headed back to a restaurant near our hotel.

Next day, it was off to the Red Fort, Red because its massive walls are built of rich red sandstone. How many acres this citadel covers I do not know, but within its walls are several palaces, harem quarters, audience halls, throne rooms, baths, etc., all surrounded by lawns and gardens.

There was a large square bath complete with thirty-two seats [all marble], where Shah Jehan would sit with his wives, while spouts of water shot into the air from fountains near their shoulders. I actually sat on the black marble throne where, after his imprisonment, Shah Jehan would sit and gaze along the Jumna at the place where his beloved Mumtaz lay at rest.

For a couple of rupees, Sandy and I joined a guide led group, composed mostly of servicemen. This proved to be a good investment, as I'm sure we would have missed a great deal. As we stood in one of the courtyards, the guide explained that behind the elaborately carved screen that enclosed three sides, was a passageway, enabling the ladies of the harem to watch and listen to the court proceedings, without being seen themselves.

The Red Fort

Another hall, where Shah Jehan would receive ambassadors and other important visitors, had a six inch deep by four feet wide channel running through it. Along the length of this channel bed there had been alternate strips of gold leaf and silver leaf, and through this trench would flow shimmering, scented water. What a wonderful spectacle this must have been, and how dignitaries must have stood in awe at all this opulence and splendour.

And so, after another arduous but rewarding day, Sandy and I returned to the leave centre. That evening, we ate at the centre restaurant, then sat by the pool sipping beer and reminiscing about all the wonderful things we had seen over the past two days.

The next morning we packed our gear, gave the bearer some baksheesh, said farewell to the reception people, and took a gharry to the station. Again, it was pandemonium trying to get into the station, never mind finding available seats. Luckily, we found a carriage occupied by some squaddies who had "reserved" a carriage for themselves. They were going much farther south than Jhansi, so when Sandy and I reached our destination, this gave them extra room to spread out.

Ernie wanted to know all about our trip, but that evening I was just too tired to talk. All I wanted to do was crawl into bed and sleep, and that came easy. I was so bushed I don't think I even showered before getting under the mosquito net, exhausted but very appreciative of what the army had given me — the opportunity to see and experience wonderful things.

Tomorrow, it was back to my section.

Chapter Fourteen
Naini Tal

The summers in Jhansi were hot and oppressive, but this all changed once the monsoon season arrived, for then it became very hot, very oppressive and very, very humid. I seem to recall the highest temperature reached was 108 degrees fahrenheit, but that was only for one day. Looking out across that flat, barren, dry, cracked surface of the miadam, one often saw small twisters of dust hurtling to who knows where. The gritty stuff got everywhere — in your socks, in your hair, up your nose, and in your ears. It was a good thing we wore shorts or trousers, or the dust may have got into even more inconvenient places.

Every day it was the same, although obviously some days were better than others. Some days there would not be a breath of wind, the air being so still it felt as if one was living in a vacuum. Other days the air was so heavy and thick [I cannot think of any other way to describe it], one felt it could be sliced with a knife. Then, once the monsoon season arrived, it was as if one had taken up residence in a Turkish bath. Needless to say, no matter what season it was, the shower stalls and dhobi wallahs were forever kept busily employed. When the first rains began to fall, fellows, including Gilbert 524, actually stripped off and stood out in the downpour, enjoying the feeling of virgin water trickling over their torsos.

It must have been sometime in late August or early September that rumours began to circulate that we might be getting 28 days leave — 28 days! Up to this point in time, all we had been granted was either a 48 or 72 hour pass, and that generally had to be tacked onto a weekend to make it worthwhile. It was all too good to be true. Never the less, everyone kept their eyes on the notice board. One week went by, then two, and half way into the third week names were actually posted, and lo and behold, there was my name, Doug's name, Sandy's name, but alas, no Sergeant Beresford. Poor old Ernie was very disappointed. So were Doug and I, that once again our little trio would not be travelling on leave together.

Ernie had a quiet word with Captain Burke, the head of his office, to see if he could swap with someone, but to no avail. It seemed the Admin Office looked after these things and would not digress from their precious rote system. He would be on the next batch, the captain told him, but still, leave without our amicable and very funny friend just wouldn't be the same. Surely there must have been someone on staff who would be willing to swap places with Ernie, but the powers that be simply would not bend the rules.

I know I have said this in a previous narrative, but there was a sort of bond between the three of us. It's difficult to describe. We had met when we were conscripted at just eighteen years of age, and had stuck together, even shared the same billets, over the past three or so years. I suppose part of it was that we were pretty naive teenagers, that we were in the army, that there was a war going on [although our little trio did no fighting, thank God], and that we were far from home. It was something I look back on with pride and also with sadness: pride, because we knew we could depend on one another; sadness, because although we kept in touch for many years after the war, our correspondence gradually came to a halt. It is something I will regret to the end of my days.

Now the big question was where to spend these four weeks? We had been to Agra and Delhi, and in any case, we wanted somewhere cool. Places like Hyderabad, Lahore with its famous Shalimar Gardens ["Pale Hands I Loved Beside the Shalimar" was a popular ballad at that time], Ootacamund [affectionately known as Ootie], and Pondicherry were much too far away and would take too many days to get there, so they were out. Darjeeling, we were told, was beautiful, and gave a wonderful view of Mount Everest, but that too meant a long train journey. Simla and Dehra Dun were also considered, but the former was the summer residence of the Viceroy, so lots of top brass would be there, and we did not fancy giving pucka salutes every five or six minutes, and as for the latter, well it was just too expensive.

Enter Sergeant Mary Grace Gidla. "Why don't you go to Naini Tal?" she said. "I've been there with my family several times, and it's very beautiful. The cost would be reasonable, and you would be able to see Nandi Devi, the third highest mountain in the world. The restaurants are good, there are a few night clubs, and there is, I think, a forces leave centre where you could stay."

Out came the maps. Mary Grace indicated where Naini Tal lay and the two or three day route, by rail and road, it would take to get there. So finally, after sorting out more information, advice, and descriptions from Mary Grace, we decided to head for the Himalayas and the summer retreat of Naini Tal. We would not regret it.

How I wished I had kept a diary of all those journeys, and especially the dates when they took place, but I didn't think of these things at the time. My feeling is that our visit to this mountainous and beautiful area took place in late September or early October of 1945.

Since the defeat of Japan, activity at GHQ 2nd echelon had slowed down quite a lot. Troops were still arriving in India but not at the same hectic rate, and, of course, some were already on troopships heading for India when the Japanese finally surrendered.

Doug, Sandy and I visited the Admin Office, and laid out our plans before the officer who looked after all leave matters. He in turn, told us he would get one of his chaps to see if there was any space available at the leave centre, and if so, make our reservations. He would also arrange for our travel documents to be issued.

Of all the people we received advice from, the majority came from a most unexpected source. For some unexplained reason, Staff Sergeant Wilson was a mine of information, not only about Naini Tal, but also concerning all the perks we could apply for. May I remind the reader, that Wilson had arrived in India as a boy soldier many years before the war started, and knew King's Regulations inside out. In short, he was one of those people known in the army as a "barrack room lawyer".

There was dhobi allowance, daily ration allowance, travel allowance, and bicycle allowance. [With a knowing smile he said, "I'm sure you'll be renting a bicycle up there, won't you?" and we played the game by replying, "Of course."] There were a couple of other little perks, but they escape me. For once in our relationship with this domineering Staff Sergeant, we sincerely thanked him, because the total amount of all these allowances paid for a great part of our trip.

Why did he do this? Well, perhaps it was his conscience digging at him, for the way he treated us when we first arrived at GHQ 2nd Echelon and upon our unexpected promotion. Maybe, it was the thought that all these temporary soldiers would soon be on their way back to the UK, leaving him to get back to his more leisurely pre-war life in New Delhi.

So there it was. Our travel plans were made, reservations confirmed, and we were off once more on another adventure. Sam Lal, my little bearer, made sure all my uniforms, underwear *etc.* were clean and pressed. The reader may recall that Sam was about 12 years old and servant to four of us Sergeants. I paid him for the coming month [actually I gave him 50% more to get himself some new shoes, finding out later that Doug had done the same thing], and told him to keep an eye on the rest of my gear, and not get into any trouble.

At around 06:00 hours we reported to the Admin Office, and collected all the necessary documents. We heaved our gear into the back of a lorry and climbed in after it. Ernie came down to see us off, and it was quite sad to be departing without him once again,

Down at Jhansi Station the RTO stamped and signed our travel warrants, then showed us to an empty carriage. We couldn't believe our luck — a whole carriage all to ourselves. The compartment, as I recall, was roughly 10 to 12 feet wide, with hinged bunks that dropped down from the wall. There were no mattresses, just wooden slats, so they were not very comfortable. One thing we were grateful for was that we had our own toilet, even though it was only a hole in the floor.

Blasts from the locomotive whistle announced our departure, and once again, a steaming giant of the Great Indian Peninsular Railway was transporting my friends and I on a new adventure towards the north of the sub-continent. I found it hard to accept that I was heading for the "roof of the world".

Shortly after the start of that memorable journey, was the first time I contemplated and dreaded the thought that sometime in the near future I would be returning to civvy street and probably factory life. After all, the war was over, and there was nothing else for all these ex-servicemen to look forward to. It was scary. How could I, now in my twenty-second year, settle down to such a boring life in a factory after all the wonderful comradeship and adventures I had experienced since joining the army? Would I, or any of us, be able to live an ordinary life again?

Anyway, here we were, clickerty-clackerting through the Indian countryside. How anything grew in this scorched earth I do not know, but there were fields of grain, corn, rice and other produce. Cows could be seen harnessed to a crude contraption that was in turn attached to a vertical wheel, upon which were lashed large open ended tins and buckets. These disappeared into a well, re-appeared full of water, and drained into a sluice, which eventually found its way onto the surrounding fields and pastures. A very primitive method of irrigation, but it worked and had done so for many centuries.

The train did pause at a few stations on the way to Lucknow, the largest city we would pass through, and it was at one of these stops that I got off to stretch my legs. To my surprise, there were some more BORs on board, and, even more of a surprise was that one of the passengers was an ATS girl. She was standing by the door, and over her head on the carriage roof was a monkey. I don't think she knew it was there, but as you can see, it was too good a photographic opportunity to miss.

Monkey on the Train to Naini Tal

Bareilly passed by in the evening dusk, as our train chugged its way north, until, in the early hours of the morning we reached the small town of Kathkadam. Outside the station an army lorry awaited to transport us holiday makers on the last part of our journey up through the Himalayan foothills to Naini Tal.

The scenery was spectacular, hair-raising at times, and very hard on the rear end. We could have only driven a few hundred yards before the road went into a series of "S" bends, then climbed at a shallow angle for a mile or so [perhaps not even that], and then it was another set of "S" bends. Sometimes it ran alongside a gentle flowing river, the other side of which was dense with trees and undergrowth, much of it rhododendrons. At places the road had been blasted out of the mountain side, so that on one side there was a sheer drop of several hundred feet.

The sepoy driver seemed not to have a care in the world as he threw the lorry around tight switchback corners, changing gears up and down and down and up, to suit the terrain. The bench seats ran along each side of the lorry,

145

so that when changing gear, with much wrenching and grinding, we would all be jostled sideways or back and forth. Every now and then, we would see three, four or five large monkeys sitting on the small wall that separated the road from the river. They sat there like little old men, watching the lorry go by, and no doubt thinking, "Who are these strange looking animals rattling down the road, invading our domain and disturbing the peace?"

Road to Naini Tal

Eventually, we came through a gap in the mountains, and there was lake Naini Tal. Another two or three miles along the lake and we at last reached our destination. Boy, were we tired. After two days on the train and the buffeting from Kathkadam, we were exhausted. The leave centre was on the next road up the mountainside, overlooking the main road and the small town at the end of the lake. The room we had was for four people, but as no-one else turned up, we had it to ourselves. The beds had freshly laundered sheets and were quite comfortable.

Legend has it that a beautiful princess was kidnapped, taken to the top of one of the peaks over-looking the lake, and murdered there. The tale relates how her eyes fell out, rolled down the mountain side, and where they came to rest two springs came to the surface and formed the lake.

Most of our days were taken up with walks along the lake-side, looking around the market, and taking it easy. One morning there was a hell of a noise going on along the main road our billet overlooked. It was a funeral, and the corpse, face uncovered and surrounded with flowers, was being carried on a bier to the ghats where it would be cremated.

Another day we witnessed a political meeting in the tiny main square. The politician was denouncing the British government, accusing them of using the Indian people as slaves and demanding independence. This was all explained to our trio by a nearby spectator who happened to be a civil servant in Naini Tal.

The next day we took the foot path that led up to China Peak [locals pronounced it Cheena Peak], and who should arrive there, being carried in a dandy, but this self-same politician who had been accusing the British of slavery. A dandy is like the sedan chair of yester-years, and after the customer takes his seat, the dandy is hoisted up from the ground by two men at the fore and two at the rear and carried to his destination. What a hypocrite!

View from China Peak

The track was terrible and steep in places and at least another five hundred feet above Naini Tal, but it was all worth the effort, as the view from China Peak was breathtaking. The scene was a broad vista of the snow-capped mountains, one of which was Nandi Devi.

On one of our morning walks, a fellow riding a horse came into view, and as he came nearer I recognized him as someone I knew from Stafford. His name was Tommy Davies, and we used to visit the same dance halls in my home town. After the war, Tommy and his Wife became champion ballroom dancers and opened their own dance school. Once again I have to say, "It's a small world."

147

Sergeant Gilbert and Tommy Davies

All too soon our Himalayan adventure drew nigh, and once again we were traveling that hazardous twisting road back to Kathkadam. A couple of hours later and we stepped onto the GIP train bound once more for Jhansi.

Chapter Fifteen
Jhansi Friends

There are friends, and then there are friends. For me, true friendship is one of the most valued assets of life. Long ago, shortly after returning to civilian life, my old scouting friend and mentor, Bill Chesworth, warned me, "Loyalty is a thing I have always tried to foster in the group, Vinnie. However, remember it can be a weakness if it is not a two way affair. Be careful, for it can cause much bitterness. You are not in the army now, where you have to rely on one another." It was good advice, because one thing I know for sure is that once my trust in someone is lost, it is generally lost forever. For me, loyalty is first and foremost.

Be that as it may, if there was one thing the army taught me, or reinforced, it was the value of true friendship. I don't mean just pals, but buddies one can count on, people who are trustworthy and dependable, like Douglas Allsop, and to a lesser degree, happy go lucky Ernest Beresford.

Obviously, no person is 100% perfect. That's an impossible thing to ask of anyone. We all have faults, and these just have to be accepted, but friendship, trust and loyalty take on a completely new meaning when one is a naive nineteen year old, who is many thousands of miles away from a home he may never see again. Oh, I know things are different now, when people think nothing of travelling to the far corners of the earth for a vacation, but before 1943, the farthest I had ever travelled from Stafford had been to London for the day, a distance of 135 miles.

Perhaps I am a bit of a romantic, but when I look back, I cannot help thinking how strange it was that on that very first NAAFI break at Shoeburyness barracks, three complete strangers, mugs of tea in hand, converged on that one particular table and within a very short time became

151

steadfast friends. Surely, the fact that we stuck together over all those years, and kept in touch for many years after the war, must say something. There was a sort of bond between us, especially after we left Britain. It was just something one had to experience.

It is my belief that as one reaches the golden years, [whoever thought up that phrase is a real comedian], it is even more important to remain loyal, even though personalities may change and may well become a bit of a bore. One meets many acquaintances in life, but the number of genuine, constant, reliable friends, can be counted on one hand, and that is if one is lucky. End of sermon.

Don't get me wrong. Most of the people I became involved with at Jhansi were also friends while we were there, but as you will see, in many cases it was only "for the duration of hostilities", a phrase often used in military documents. Once our service together was over, so was the friendship. It was only to be expected really.

Among the many characters I came into contact with at Jhansi, Britons like Sapper Chappel, Sergeants Stout, Harry Mason, Sandy Harris, Steve Taylor, RSM Hedley Arblaster, plus the unforgettable Miss Woof [yes, that was her real name], are worth mentioning.

On the Indian side, there was Bala Singh, Mary Grace Gidla, and Sheik Mohammad Lukfor Rahman [SML Rahman, for short].

How the trio of Doug, Ernie, and myself gradually increased in numbers, is clouded over now, but gradually Hedley, Eddie, Stouty, Sandy, Steve and Harry joined us. Although we all worked in different offices, we nearly always sat together in the Sergeant's Mess, except for Eddie. He was a Sapper [Private in the Royal Engineers], and so had to eat in another mess because of ridiculous army rules. Eddie worked with Stouty, under Hedley, and I suppose this is how we all got acquainted.

Don't get the idea that we went around in a big gang. No, it was more a case of, "Doug and I are going to the cinema tonight, who's coming?" Most evenings three, four or five of us would congregate for a chinwag in one or the other's basher while sipping mugs of Syed Wazir Ali's evil tasting char [no NAAFI east of Suez]. Poor old Sandy always joined us for the Saturday night "dances", except for when he was in hospital. Harry didn't dance, but would generally join us for a film or a visit to a restaurant in Sadar Bazaar. If a special trip came up, or if we were granted leave, we would try and arrange it so two or three of us could go together. That is how Doug and I managed to visit Datia and Naini Tal together, and Steve Taylor and I to see Agra.

An establishment like GHQ 2nd Echelon India Command was a great mixer of personalities. One only had to listen to Hedley and Steve to know they were well educated, but to what level I did not know. Stout and Sandy had attended local grammar schools, whilst Doug had been educated at Doctor Barnardo's home in Ilford, Essex. Harry had attended St. Mongo's Academy in Glasgow. Me? Well, at the age of 14, I graduated from that noble, spacious, well-appointed academy of higher learning, St. Patrick's Roman Catholic Senior School [3 classrooms, 3 teachers].

Confidence was a thing I lacked when I joined the army, and now, here at Jhansi, I really felt inferior, listening and absorbing all that was going on around me. However, this changed somewhat when, to my utter surprise, I was promoted from Gunner directly up to Sergeant. Little by little, the comprehension came that I had performed as well as, and even better, in the examinations than some of my learned friends. It also made me aware that I was capable of more than just standing behind a centre lathe at the English Electric Co. Ltd. factory in my home town. The education I received at Jhansi, by observing and listening to all that went on in the office and mess, was something that could never be duplicated, and was worth its weight in gold.

Having said all that, here is a short precis of some of my Jhansi pals and others. My only problem is how to paint a picture in words of this diverse bunch of people who were my constant companions for three years or more, but I will try.

Sergeant Stout

Stouty was a first-rate athlete, a strong swimmer, enjoyed playing chess, and overall was fun to be with. He had an uncommon name that escapes me, but it was something biblical, like Ebenezer or Zechariah;,names that did not suit him at all, for he was definitely not a scrooge, nor was he religious.

Sergeant Stout, a native of Manchester, had an enormous nose, and was the butt of many jokes, which he always took in good part. One joke was that if he ever entered a race, he could always win by a nose. Sometimes, when he entered the Sergeants' Mess, some of the lads would sing, "No Nose [Rose] in All the World, Until You Came" or "Tis the Last Nose [Rose] of Summer", first lines of popular ballads of that time. On these occasions he would halt, let the door close behind him, then throw up his arms and acknowledge the welcome. I liked Stouty.

Sapper Eddie Chappel

Sapper Edward Chappel of the Royal Engineers was a fellow I really admired. He had endured more than a year of horrific and exhausting combat in the jungles of Burma against the Japanese and had been present at the Battle of Kohima. I admired him because he was a reliable, sincere, intelligent and quite humble man for what he had been through. There was also another battle of a different sort that he would have to face when he returned home to England.

You see, as a member of the pre-war Part-Time Territorial Army [reserve], Eddie was called up to the colours right at the beginning of the war in September of 1939, and a few months later he was shipped out to India. Why India, Eddie could never understand, for it was reasonably peaceful in the far east at that time, except for the Japanese invasion of china. It would be another two years before Japan would attack the British Empire and the USA.

When one is very young, one gets all sorts of silly naive romantic notions about war and love, and so before proceeding overseas, he and his eighteen year old girlfriend decided they wanted to get married, even though parents on both sides tried to talk them out of it. And so it came as quite a shock, when three months later, he received a letter telling him he was going to be a daddy. I felt really sorry for Eddie, because when he did eventually return home, his little boy was nearly six years old.

In a letter posted to me after he had been repatriated, he related what a terrible time he was having, trying to get to know his son. Throughout those war years, there had been just the boy and his mother, and then suddenly this complete stranger walked into the house and became the object of his mother's affection and head of the family. Not only that, but Eddie also had to get to know his wife all over again. Six years is a long time to be separated, and obviously, because of their different wartime experiences, they had both changed in so many ways. It must have been heart breaking.

About a year or so later, he stopped writing, so I never did find out if the family reunion was a success or not, and so after a couple of more letters, with no reply, I gave up. Eddie often talked about immigrating to New Zealand after the war, and he probably did, because from the tone of his last few letters it was plain the reunion had not been a success, and the marriage was on the rocks. It's sad. He was such a good and caring fellow.

Alas, there were thousands of similar cases of servicemen and women returning to civilian life, only to find their marriages in ruins and divorce the only solution. Many of these lonely, long separated wives, had met and fallen for someone else, especially Americans and Canadians, and wanted to end their marriages as soon as possible.

The same applied to the menfolk. Thousands of servicemen returned home, only to inform their spouse or fiancé that they had met someone else

Sapper Eddie Chappel

with whom they wanted to spend the rest of their lives. Some fellows didn't even bother to come home. They just stayed with their new found loves in Italy, South Africa, Kenya, Singapore, or wherever they happened to be stationed. Hundreds just immigrated with their new wives directly to places like Canada, New Zealand or Australia. Staff Sergeant Wilson stayed in India. You see, a fellow could choose where he wished to be demobilized — Blighty or Timbuktu.

After peace broke out, there was much finger pointing, with remarks like, "She messed around with a Yank, Aussie, Norwegian or Pole," or "He had a bit of stuff in Brussels, New Delhi, Cairo or Bournemouth." When I look back on those terrible war years, many servicemen and women didn't know if they would ever see their homeland again. Somewhere, every day and every night, bombs, V1 and V2 rockets, shells, bullets, and disease were killing civilians and combatants alike. It may have been morally wrong, but I personally cannot find it in my heart to condemn these fellow human beings.

All over that drab, blacked out shattered world, in those places where death and danger was a constant companion, an oft repeated quote was, "Live for today for I may not be here tomorrow." This was particularly true of bomber crews. Who can blame those brave young men and teenagers for seeking love and affection? I certainly do not. It is all too easy for anyone who didn't live through those brutal years and see at first hand the daily sight of death, the turmoil and combat of war, to point a finger and make heartless and cruel remarks.

A prime example of the lasting effects of what those young men went through is my step-daughter Lesley's father-in-law, Tom Donaldson of Sidney, Vancouver Island, Canada. He died at the ripe old age of 88, but this ex-RCAF Lancaster Navigator took part in 32 bomber raids over Germany, one of the few to survive a complete tour of duty, which is what 32 missions was called. Because of this nerve shattering ordeal, even in his advanced years, he suffered from terrible nightmares and would awake in the depths of night screaming. Can you honestly tell me it was wrong for any of these brave youthful heroes, for that is what they were, to seek out a little female companionship?

The casualties, anguish, and heartbreaks of the war did not cease on VE or VJ Day. Divorces, desertions, and meaningless marriages kept together only because of the children were commonplace. Marriages between 18 and 19 year olds with glorious and silly romantic ideas about war would never have taken place in more sensible times. It was, to quote Dickens, "The best of times and the worst of times."

Chappel had served in every campaign in Burma until a few months earlier, when he was severely wounded and sent back to a hospital in India. He would never talk about action in the jungle, except once he told me, "It was vicious, and most of the time I was bloody well terrified. All I want to do is get home and try to forget about it all." I don't suppose any of those who experienced the real savagery of war will ever forget it. I never referred to the subject again.

Eddie worked under Hedley Arblaster, so whilst on duty it was "Sapper Chappel" and "Sergeant Major Arblaster, Sir", but when out together it was Eddie and Hedley. This was the difference between being behind a desk and being behind a gun.

Then came the time when, after successfully passing the final exams, Douglas, Ernie and I were promoted to Sergeant. This meant more money, which was all very nice. However, it also caused a bit of a problem, because Eddie was still receiving a Private's pay. To get over this, whenever we visited a bar or restaurant, Hedley would obtain the bill, and arrange things so that Eddie paid very much less than we did, the difference being shared between the remainder of us later. I'm sure he guessed what was going on, but wisely never questioned it. Everyone liked Eddie, and as you may have guessed, he and I became good friends. If he's still alive, I wonder where he is today.

Staff Sergeant Wilson.

As I've already stated, Wilson was the one who really ran the section. He knew the King's Regulations and procedures like the back of his hand. He would quote excerpts from them as if he was reading the Bible.

The toughest part of my work was getting paperwork past Wilson's critical eye, as he always seemed to take great pleasure from pointing out mistakes. It was destructive, not constructive criticism. However, after about five or six months of this, a most unusual thing happened, and I was able to turn the tables on him.

One day he took me outside of the office, and I thought, "What the hell have I done now?" After a few questions like, "How do you like it here?" and "What do you think of India?" he finally got round to the real reason for our little tete-a-tete. He was short of money, and wanted me to loan him something like 200 rupees, [later I found out he was a heavy gambler, a no-no in the army].

What a dilemma! If I didn't lend him the money, he would make my life hell, and yet the last thing I wanted to do was help him out. In the end, I said I would let him have the money tomorrow, but I wanted the transaction in his own handwriting, signed and dated. About a week later, when he was going over one of my letters, quaking in my shoes, I casually, and in the most friendly and confidential way, mentioned that according to King's Regulations the borrowing of money is a chargeable offence, especially when the borrower is someone of higher rank. I quietly pointed out to him that we had both better keep very quiet about our little IOU, or we would both be in hot water. I pointed out to him that if Captain Curzon ever found out, Wilson would be up for a courts martial and would most probably be reduced to the ranks. Looking back, I just cannot believe I had the nerve to do what I did, but I had thought it all out and knew Wilson would take the hint that I had something over on him.

That night, when I related to Doug what I had done, he looked aghast at me and gasped, "Bloody hell!" Then after a long silence, he asked, "What in heaven's name did you do that for? You and I are really in for it now."

Believe me, the action I had taken was the cause of much personal anguish, and a few sleepless nights, but thankfully, Doug was wrong. From that day onwards, we were treated more fairly. Sergeant Grubb must have noticed the change in attitudes, because he also became more friendly and helpful.

RSM Hedley Arblaster

There is infantry, light infantry, and motorized infantry, and Regimental Sergeant Major Hedley Arblaster, of the Royal Worcestershire Regiment, was part of the group that dealt with all three. What he did before the war I do not know, but he was an excellent organizer and highly intelligent. Stouty, who also worked in the same office, told me Hedley was a much more accomplished administrator than the officer in charge of that section.

Although it was obvious he had received a much better education than myself, and his family were quite wealthy and in a social level very much higher than my own family, he was not in the least snobbish. It was hinted that Hedley had in fact attended the public school known as Marlborough College, which is one of the elite colleges of Britain. He always treated everyone the same, except for one person — Arthur Jones, but then sadly, I cannot think of anyone who liked this egotist.

Hedley was a very good warrant officer, being patient and understanding when dealing with a difficult situation. Although I was not in his office, he knew I was having trouble with Sergeant Grubb and would coach me on how to deal with him. I point this out because there were some, like Grubb, who really tried to act like superior beings.

Hedley's brother happened to be the Commanding Officer of Embarkation

Headquarters, Bombay, so when peace was declared and Hedley was granted twenty-eight days leave, he decided to take the long journey south [three days] and spend time with his brother. A nice and very natural thing to do, you may say. Ah, but this presented a very large predicament.

Sergeants Gilbert and Mason, and RSM Arblaster

Hedley was a WO1, a BOR [British Ordinary Rank], but his big brother was a full blown Colonel, and King's Regulations state that a BOR cannot dine in the Officers' Mess and vice versa. The problem was resolved by Hedley borrowing one of his brother's subalterns uniform. In this way, they could travel around and visit clubs as Colonel and Lieutenant Arblaster. Because of this ridicules rule, they both could have been courts martialled, Hedley for masquerading as an officer, and his brother for aiding and abetting.

Hedley was also the proud possessor of a six pounder anti-tank shot, [the one inch diameter by six inches long pointed armour piercing chunk of metal that actually strikes the target], and this he used a paper weight. Miss Woof, one of only four English ATS girls on the camp, also happened to work in his office. I cannot think of her first name, because she was always referred to as plain Miss Woof.

Sometimes, when Miss Woof reported to Hedley's desk, he would place his fingers around the shot moving them up and down in a stroking manner, look her straight in the eyes and ask, "Is there anything I can do for you Miss Woof?" She would turn a vivid crimson colour, slam down any papers, or ask her question as quickly as possible, then make a hasty, embarrassing retreat.

Naturally, we all had a good laugh over this antic.

There was a special guard on the ATS quarters at night, but this did not stop some officers from making nocturnal visits. They were not bad looking girls, but neither were they raving beauties. In one issue of the ALFSEA weekly newspaper, a cartoon depicted a great fat ugly ATS girl surrounded by dozens of soldiers, and the balloon coming out of her mouth said, "I didn't realize how attractive I was until I came to India." Actually, I thought the cartoon was rather heartless and uncalled for.

When Hedley left Jhansi to be de-mobbed, we never heard from him again.

Sergeant Harry "Jock" Mason

Harry, a Scot from Kilmarnock had the next bed to mine. He was also a good Catholic, whatever that means, and always dragged me off to Mass on Sunday mornings. The garrison church was just like an old stone country church back home in England, and those attending were servicemen from all over the British Isles, plus Australians, West Africans, Ghurkhas, Anglo Indians, and Indians. The priest was French. The Mass was celebrated in Latin, consequently it was quite impressive to see all these people of different nationalities and colours following the service with the aid of the Missal.

Harry was quite a gifted footballer [soccer player] too, and had tried out for Glasgow Celtic a few weeks before joining the army. Whether he played for any of the big teams after the war, I do not know, because, even though I wrote to him twice, he never replied. I couldn't understand why. We had been close friends, so it was very disappointing.

Tommy Lawton, a well-known and popular Arsenal and England footballer of that time, was given the task of organising a team of moral boosting peacetime professionals whose job it was to tour India and play games against local unit teams. The team was in fact, called Tommy Lawton's Eleven. Harry was picked to play centre half for GHQ 2nd Echelon, and after the game Lawton came over and congratulated him on an excellent game. Obviously, the Lawton team did not play to their generally high international standard, especially on a playing surface that was sun-baked clay, devoid of any grass. I can't remember the result, but our side's performance was nothing to be ashamed of.

Tommy Lawton's Eleven also played a team from a battalion of the West African Frontier Force, who were stationed nearby. Some of these coloured soldiers played in bare feet and were really no match for the English team. Great cheers would erupt from the WAFF team supporters whenever one of their players kicked the ball high. It didn't matter that the ball went to an

English player, so long as it flew high in the sky. It was quite hilarious.

Sergeant Steven Taylor

There are many things I could say to describe Steve Taylor, but the word "smart" says it all. A native of Walsall, only a few miles from my own home town, he was clever, always well groomed, and amazingly, did not possess that terrible Black Country accent.

Steve, with his neatly trimmed Errol Flynn moustache and polished confident speech and manner, gave me the impression he came from a family with money, and had enjoyed a good education at a public school, [Shrewsbury, I think] away from his hometown. Steve also had left wing socialist and communist ideals, and from little snippets he would drop now and again, I got the feeling one of his teachers had encouraged these far left views.

Before the war there was no such thing as the National Health Scheme. In addition, the opportunity to obtain a university or even a grammar school education was slim for anyone from a poor family. This I know from personal experience.

Occasionally, in the mess or bar, politics would rear its ugly head, and believe me the discussions were long, heated, but never bitter. I was pretty innocent about these matters, so kept quiet and just listened and absorbed the various arguments. At times like this, I felt somewhat inadequate and extremely ignorant about the world of politics. Quite frankly, because we just accepted it, I had never given much thought about the existing class structure in Britain. It was yet another chapter in my worldly education, and I relished it. I have to admit that I did put my proverbial foot in my mouth a couple of times until I learned when to keep quiet.

Taylor never made great long speeches or raised his voice, but his subtle remarks always hit the mark. For instance, I recall a discussion about how only people with money could get the best hospital treatment. He just said, "Why should a Lord's son get better treatment than your son? They're both human beings. They're both British. They both contribute to the country, and both are precious to their families. So why should there be one treatment for the rich and another for the poor?"

On education, he would state something similar like, "What makes you think that the Prime Minister's son is any brainier or deserves a better education than a labourer's son? Just because a chap has had the luck to be born into a wealthy class society, doesn't mean he's intelligent or will become a genius." Short statements like this made me and many others ponder over his words, and think, "Yes, there is something in what he says. Why should there be a difference?"

Referring to class distinction, he once remarked, "Have you never noticed what an important part accents play in British films? Take the film, *In Which We Serve*. All the officers have frightfully posh accents from Cambridge, Oxford, Eton or Winchester, while all the lower ranks have Cockney, Broad Lancashire, Scottish, or Shropshire farmers' brogues." I must confess, I hadn't noticed, but I didn't let Steve know this, and of course, he was right, as anyone who has seen the film will know.

The books he read were nearly always biographies, autobiographies, or politics. One day, in the mess, there was just Ernie, Steve and myself, when the conversation got around to Ghandi, who had been much in the news of late. Up to this point, I had never really thought much about him, but it was Steve's opinion that he was one the greatest men on this earth. As great a philosopher in the east as Bertrand Russell was in the west. Who, I pondered, was Bertrand Russell?

To me, Mahatma Ghandi had been that pathetic little, dhoti clad figure seen on newsreels, living among the untouchables [India's lowest caste], and leading non-violent protest marches throughout India against British rule. The British government had imprisoned him several times, branding him a troublemaker, but to Steve, he was only demanding what was right for his country. Of course, Steve was right, and after learning more about the man I agreed with him, Ghandi was one the giants of the 20th century.

Once he said something I have never forgotten and apply even to this day. "I always try to turn the question around," he said. "For instance, when there's a large protest march in Bombay, I ask myself, 'How would the people of Birmingham react if Indian troops occupied Britain, and the British people were forced to buy only goods that were manufactured in India?'."

That really gave me food for thought. Steve was full of short, straight to the point statements like this. Up to this point, I had not realized that Britain had captive markets in the sub-continent and many of its colonies. Only cloth imported from Britain was allowed to be sold in India. No wonder cities like Manchester prospered. One way in which Ghandi protested against British rule was by weaving his own cloth for his own dhoti, and encouraging all those Indians who could to do likewise. He, in fact created a nationwide cottage industry.

Steve and I were friends, but not close friends, even though we took trips and attended dances together. Like so many wartime acquaintances, we never saw or contacted each other after demobilization.

Sergeants Gilbert and Taylor

Sergeant Sandy Harris

To be honest, I cannot recall a great deal about this tall blonde native of Peterborough, except that he was one of the nicest fellows I have ever met. He was charming, compassionate and good company. One thing I do remember is that the poor chap spent a lot of time in hospital, recuperating from terrible bouts of malaria, and was once stricken down with dysentery.

The battle with dysentery left him a physical wreck, and his condition came as a devastating shock when I visited him in hospital. He looked so haggard and drained I really thought he was near death. His appearance during the recurring bouts of malaria was equally dreadful. The perspiration would be pouring out of him as he lay under the mosquito net. His face was yellow, his head would roll from side to side, and every now and again, his body would vibrate with a sort of giant shiver. It was awful to watch, and when he was particularly bad, I would just sit by his bed for ten or so minutes and leave feeling very upset.

Each day, Sandy took doses of mepacrine, [this caused his complexion to have a yellowish tinge], to control the malaria, but the disease never leaves you once it has been contracted. Incidentally, after sundown, it was compulsory to wear long trousers and long sleeved shirts, but one could be bitten by a disease bearing insect any time. It was just the luck of the draw.

Sandy and I went on many trips together including Agra, and the hill station of Naini Tal.

Sergeant Arthur Jones

I'm sure the reader has met someone whom you instantly disliked. It's unfortunate, but like many others, I could not take to Arthur. There was something about him that rattled 99% of the chaps with whom he came into contact. He was always smartly turned out, but he was so arrogant, so self-opinionated, so bigoted and so nasty tempered and, I am reluctant to say, so very efficient. When he walked, he had a sort of bounce in his step, as if to say, "I'm better than any of you lot."

Sometimes, when sitting in the bar or mess, someone would look up and say, "Uh, oh, here comes Jonesy to join us." Immediately a moan would travel around the table, and many times Hedley and others would get up and leave. I don't think I have ever known someone so antisocial, and so unpopular.

Oddly enough, he came from the same district, Stoke-on-Trent, as Ernie Beresford, but that's the only thing they had in common. Although they were both from the Potteries, they were completely different. Ernie was extremely

Sergeant Sandy Harris

popular, Arthur, sad to say, unbearable.

Sergeant Ernest Beresford

What can one say about a character such as Ernie? Certainly, fellows like him are few and very far between. This comrade was devil may care, a real comedian, a beautiful dancer, had an attractive personality and was women crazy. Above all, he was, with Doug Allsop, my good and faithful companion from that fateful first day at Shoeburyness Barracks, until I left Jhansi bound for home sweet home. There was about him that certain something one cannot put a finger on, that made him so amiable. With a long chin and mischievous smile, he was not particularly good looking. In fact, he was the spitting image of that great comedian, Tommy Handley.

Ernie was probably the most popular fellow in the unit, not only with the men but also with the few ladies around. In England, there had been plenty of girls, but out here, available women were as scarce as hens' teeth and nearly always heavily chaperoned. Yet somehow, after only a short time, there he was up to his old tricks. Hedley reckoned that Ernie could talk the panties off a Mother Superior, and he was probably right.

I've known many people in my life who were good at ad libbing, but Ernie topped them all. He used to have us in stitches with his jokes and funny cracks, particularly when relating some of his amorous adventures. He was engaged to a girl back home, but somehow I couldn't see him settling down and being a faithful husband. Whoever he married was in for a rough ride, but one never knows, does one?

There was one incident, when the whole basher thought he was really in deep trouble. No, it did not take place in the bedroom, but on the parade ground. It happened like this.

About every six months or so, guard duty had to be performed, and everyone had to take their turn, from CSMs down. This entailed handling a rifle with live ammunition. Well, off went Ernie to the parade ground in front of the Admin Office where the discipline RSM, a regular soldier from the Royal Inniskilling Fusiliers, and the duty officer awaited to inspect the guard.

This RSM was army mad. It was his life. He was always impeccably turned out, with not a thing out of place. Not only that, but he also wore puttees, not gaiters like the rest of us. Puttees were like long khaki bandages that one wound around ones legs from the boots to just below the knee. They had not been used in the British Army since way before the war. We could spot him a mile away, because of his manner, his gait, and the yellow heckle he wore on his pith helmet or bush hat.

Sergeant Ernest Beresford

Let me explain that when the guard is paraded for inspection, the duty officer or the RSM examines each rifle to ensure it is clean and in good service order. Live bullets are placed in the magazine, and upon the appropriate order, the soldier works the bolt of the rifle backwards and forwards until all five rounds have been ejected. He then points the weapon forward at about forty-five degrees and pulls the trigger. This ensures no bullet is left in the breach when the rifle is inspected. The soldier is supposed to count the rounds as they fly from the breach, but alas, poor Sergeant Beresford did not.

Imagine the guard all lined up, and the necessary order given to start the drill. Bolts start flashing backwards and forwards, and shells start soaring through the air onto the ground. Rifles are presented forward, triggers pulled, and lo and behold, a bullet screams past the RSM's head and embeds itself in the side of the Admin Office. From the recoil of the one rifle, it was obviously from Ernie's gun. Immediately he is placed under close arrest and marched off to a guard room cell.

When word of this calamity reached the basher, Doug and I walked round to the rear of the guard room to commiserate with him through the barred window. He was really worried. This time he was definitely for the high jump. This time he was surely going to end up in Lucknow Kunji House [military prison], but surprise, surprise, just before tiffin next day, who should walk into the office, all smiles and smelling of roses, but good old Ernie.

"What happened?" we asked.

"I got charged with wasting the king's ammunition and have to take on extra duties for the next month."

How lucky can one get? He nearly kills the RSM and all gets is extra duties. It could only happen to one Ernest Beresford.

We kept in touch for many years after the war, but then like all the others, contact gradually slipped away. To this day, I do not know if he ever got married, or if he changed. How I wish we were still pals.

Sergeant Douglas Allsop

No one was a more reliable buddy than Doug. How he came to spend most of his life in Doctor Barnardo's orphanage home I do not know, nor did I inquire. He could not remember his parents, so he must have been a small baby when taken into the orphanage. Ernie and I were the only ones privy to this information. It was enough for me to have him as a companion. Perhaps it was his orphanage upbringing that made him such an excellent chum.

Doug was quiet, sensible, and very logical. He never joined in the arguments that went on in the mess, but one could see the cogs turning over in his brain. I don't know what else to say about him, except that he had a very large Adam's apple.

Sergeants Gilbert and Allsop

I mentioned earlier that he did find a long lost aunt, and she had offered him a home after hostilities had ceased. It worked out okay, I'm happy to say, but again after many years, we lost touch.

Doug and Ernie are the two fellows I miss most from those long ago years. There is one other, Alf Welin, who I served with at Kinston-on-Thames and Bradford. I wonder what they did with their lives, and if they are still alive?

Sergeant Bala Singh

There were about ten Indian havildars in the X-1 Office, some were Hindu, some were Muslim, and one a Christian. A Maharatti, Bala Singh was tubby, five foot six tall and ugly, but it was a nice and likeable ugliness, if you know what I mean. It was rarely that he did not have a large broad smile upon his face, showing a mouthful of gleaming uneven teeth.

Although his name was Singh, he was not a Sikh. In fact, it was he who pointed out to me, "All Sikhs are Singhs, but all Singhs are not Sikhs." Oddly enough, he was a favourite of Staff Sergeant Wilson, and was often consulted by him and Captain Curzon when there were problems with the other havildars. They all spoke good English, but sometimes they would try to be awkward, especially SLM Rahman.

When my brother's small son Brian was nearing his birthday, I wrote on a sheet of paper, "Happy birthday from your uncle Vin." Then, with the aid of "His Ugliness", I went around the office asking havildars to convert this message into their own native dialect or language. Unbelievably, there were about twelve different interpretations.

Towards the end of the war, there was a lot of talk about India gaining independence from Britain. Some, mostly Moslims, wanted our troops to depart as quickly as possible after the armistice; others did not want the British to leave at all. One of these was Bala Singh. He said to me one day, that while the British were here there would be law, order and justice, but once we left, wholesale slaughter, bribery and corruption would prevail. History proved him correct, because that is exactly what took place when Pakistan separated from India. Trains arrived in India from Pakistan with carriages full of hacked to death Hindu passengers, and the same applied to Muslims who tried to migrate to Pakistan.

Bala Singh had leadership qualities, and I am happy to report, that just before I left Jhansi, he had been accepted for OCTU [Officer Cadet Training Unit]. As you may have guessed, I liked "His Ugliness".

Sheik Mohamid Lukfer Rahman

Why this six feet tall, swarthy, handsome, Bengali Muslim volunteered for the Indian Army is beyond me. He not only hated the British, but also anything and everything related to the Hindu religion, no matter how slight. This being so, he was an enthusiastic supporter of Mohammed Jinnah [leader of the Muslim Congress], who was agitating for the partition of India into two separate states.

How Rahman got away with some of his actions, I will never know. There was not a week went by without Bala Singh and he having heated arguments. He should have been either placed on a charge or transferred elsewhere, preferably back to Bengal.

Sergeant Mary Grace Gidla

Mary Grace, as everyone called her, was a small, quiet, diminutive, Indian Church of England Christian. She was always neatly dressed in a khaki sari and seemed to float along when she walked, and since she was such a graceful little thing, her name suited her. The only other thing I can recall about Mary Grace is that her lawyer father was yet another who was not looking forward to independence and the departure of the British Raj.

Was India 70 years ago? How time flies. Where are all these ghosts from the past now? What did they do with their lives? It's strange to think that such a diverse and motley band of teenagers and young men were thrown together in that manner, and then after demobilization, just vanished and scattered around the UK and probably the world, like dust in the wind. How many, I wonder, are still alive, and do any one of them remember Royal Artillery Sergeant Vinnie Gilbert 524, as I remember them?

Chapter Sixteen
The Beginning of The End

Suddenly, on the 15 August 1945, it was announced that the Japanese had unconditionally surrendered, after two new types of bomb had been dropped on their cities with devastating results. We just couldn't believe it. Everyone was clapping everyone else on the back, cheering and whooping it up. Soon the offices were emptying as we all headed for the Mess and the bar. The feeling was indescribable. One didn't know whether to cry, scream, shout or sing, it was all so fantastic. The Mess bar was kept busy well into the night, and when all had drifted back to their bashers, it was with a great sense of relief that they lost consciousness and drifted into happy and contented sleep.

With the war finally over, we all knew repatriation back to the United Kingdom and demobilization would be coming, but no-one knew when. In fact, one could choose where the process took place. Many chose countries like New Zealand, Australia and Canada. Some even chose to stay in India.

Every member of the armed forces was given a Demobilization Group Number, starting with number one for the longest serving soldier, sailor or airman, and so it was that my good friend Sapper Eddie Chappel was the first to leave, having been in the East for six long years. Eddie was the 'Old Man' of our little group, being the ripe old age of twenty-five. The same arrangement also applied to the women who had served in the ATS, WAAF, and the WRENS. However, in some cases, servicemen were allowed to jump the queue on compassionate grounds [ie. a member of the family near to death].

It was time to leave India. In fact, it was time for all British forces to leave India, which they did just a few years later. No people want to see foreign troops walking around their country, even if they are friendly occupiers. I can honestly state that in all my time there, I did not experience any hostile actions towards or from native people. I had not carried a firearm, except for Guard Duty, all the time I was there, and I had been in some very strange places indeed.

There had been riots, mostly in Bombay and Calcutta, where troops had been called out to restore order, but these upheavals occurred when Muslim and Hindu zealots clashed with one another. Yet another case of religion rearing its ugly head, and as history would show, when independence finally arrived, the Muslim Congress demanded their country of Pakistan.

Unlike some colonial powers, the British left India with a fully functioning civil service, manned by Indians at all levels, so the hand-over was quite smooth. Unfortunately the same cannot be said of Pakistan, which is still in turmoil to this day, and as Bala Singh foretold, there was the most terrible slaughter of Muslims and Hindus who happened to live on the wrong side of the new border lines.

Saying farewell to Eddie was bitter-sweet, and yet it was wonderful to think he would soon be reunited with his wife, and would be able to hold in his arms the little boy he had only seen in photographs. As I have already related in the chapter about Jhansi friends, the reunification turned out to be a complete disaster and the marriage eventually ended in divorce.

After waving my friend goodbye, I began to think about what I was going to do with my life in the years ahead. What was I going back to? I dreaded the thought of returning to work in the English Electric Ltd. factory again, and in my case, who was to say there would be a job waiting for me there. The reader should remember that hundreds of thousands of returning service men and women would also be looking for employment.

How would I readjust to life within a building with little natural light and with noise created by great pieces of machinery, when for the past few years I had, more or less, been living in the open air? Also, I knew I was capable of doing more than just standing behind a centre lathe all day, every day. I had associated with and learned from men who had been educated at some of Britain's greatest schools, such as Shrewsbury and Marlborough. I had been the guest of a Maharajah and been to the roof of the world. I had a bearer to make my bed, clean my uniform and brasses, and take my laundry to the dhobi wallah. In the Sergeants Mess, meals and drinks had been served to me by uniformed waiters. I had seen wonderful and amazing sights, and the scope of my world had reached unforeseen horizons. It really worried me.

How I would have fared if I had seen real action and fighting I do not know, and luckily I did not have to find out. Be that as it may, I just could not see myself in front of a troop of gunners, yelling and ordering them to open fire on the enemy, or taking part in a bayonet charge. The Manningham Lane instructor had declared, "If it's you or him, you will do it," but that was not for me, and I'm just glad I didn't have to find out if I could really do it. As it was, I had walked into Copthorne Barracks as a naive private, and now sometime in the near future I would be returning to my hometown as a worldly sergeant.

I owed the army a lot. It had taught me discipline, conformity to rules, everything in its place and a place for everything. It taught me to study and concentrate on a subject until I was satisfied with the final result. Through the army, I had received a wonderful education and experienced a world I never knew existed when I boarded the train from Stafford to Shrewsbury.

The weeks and months following Eddie's departure crawled by. Back at X1 section, names that one somehow vaguely remembered from the past began to reappear in correspondence again, stating they belonged to Demob Group 'X' and were being transferred to the same transit camp that had welcomed my friends and me into India, only now it was called, Homeward Bound Trooping Depot, or HBTD.

Obviously we all talked about what might lie ahead. Doug, I'm happy to say, was going to live with his newly found aunt in Newbury, Berkshire, but he hadn't a clue what he was going to do with the rest of his life. As for the irrepressible Ernest Beresford, he hadn't got a clue either, but I'm sure that even if he fell into a load of cow manure, he would come up smelling of roses.

Our four ATS girls, including the unforgettable Miss Woof, were shipped out quite early, only to serve the remainder of their enlistment time in the UK.

Gradually our numbers dwindled, the vacated positions, where required, being taken over by Indian officers and havidars. Many departed promising to keep in touch, but few did. Regimental Sergeant Major Hedly Arblaster and Sergeant Steven Wilson didn't bother to make such a request. They simply came around, shook hands and said goodbye. These two fellows had taught me so much that I was at a loss for words. I remember saying to Hedly, "Goodbye, and thanks for your help." He reached out, patted me on the shoulder and replied, "Take care of yourself, Vinnie, and don't forget to keep your head down." Isn't it strange how one recalls things like that?

Then the fateful day came when I was called to the Admin Office. It was a day I both welcomed and dreaded: welcomed, because I would be reunited with my family once more, and dreaded, because I was afraid of what the future held, but there it was in black and white. In three days, after more bitter-sweet farewells, I would climb aboard a train bound for HBTD Deolali.

It was here that I met three sergeants from the Parachute Regiment, one of whom was quite a nutty character. His father, I was told, was the Lord Lieutenant of some large Scottish city, but Wilson, [yet another Wilson], had decided to remain in the army and had accepted an invitation to attend an Officer cadet Training Unit in the UK.

One day another sergeant entered our basher and inquired in a very, very posh voice, "I say, any of you chaps going to OCTU? What?"

Wilson replied, "Yes, I'm attending the college."

Whereupon our visitor held out his hand to shake, stating rather haughtily, "Good show. My name is Humphrey George Albert John Fortescue-Smythe [or something of that nature]. What's yours?"

Wilson replied, "Tug", and we all broke up with laughter. For those readers who may be unaware about British nicknames, Wilsons for some unknown reason always seem to get labeled with the nickname of "Tug".

Some of the tales the other two related about this Tug Wilson were bizarre. If what they told me was true I don't know how he got selected to be an officer. Perhaps in the parachute regiment they needed this mad type of leader.

Whereas all troops had one kit bag, Tug had purloined one extra, which I was led to believe, was full of 'booty'. He would tie the two kit bags together and place them so one lay across his chest and the other draped across his back. This accomplished, one of the one of the other sergeants would hand him his rifle, plus a small suitcase and other bits. Tug would charge up and down, practicing how he would get all his extra gear on board ship. You see, one could take aboard only what one could carry. It was hilarious.

About a week later it was back on the train, down to Bombay and there to embark on the *SS Chitral.* This was a 16,500 ton troopship and traveled much faster than the *Johann de Witte.* In fact, I think the smooth and uneventful voyage took only sixteen or seventeen days to reach Southampton.

Home — well nearly home, at last. The dockside was crowded with people waving and shouting to the newly returned servicemen. One squaddie near me was heard to say, "Boy, aren't they pale?" Deck by deck the ship gave up its passengers, as they walked down the gangway, through an adjacent building and onto a train that would take them up to Waterloo Station, London.

From somewhere, a voice I recognized as Tug Wilson's bellowed out, "Look out below!" and down, flying through the air came one large kit bag, scattering everyone on the dockside, and again Tug's voice, "Keep an eye on that for me fellows, will you?"

The *SS Chitral*

My orders, as were many others, were to report to a camp in Thetford, Norfolk. It was a Thursday evening when I arrived, and I was just shown to a billet and told all documentation would be taken care of next day. However it was late afternoon on that Friday before my turn came, and then I was given the news that I would have to wait till Monday before proceeding to the York Demob Centre. They didn't work on weekends.

I thought, "To hell with this," so I asked if I could have my travel documents, *etc.* and make my own way there. Damn it, but I wasn't going to hang around there when I could get home to my family. Reluctantly they agreed, but even then, for some reason I could not get away from Thetford before Saturday afternoon.

On the way to Euston Railway Station in London, I pondered how I could let my family know that I would be arriving in Stafford late that night. What was I to do? People didn't have phones in their houses like they do today. I decided to try and contact the Telegraph Public House on Wolverhampton Road and ask if they would pass on a message to my parents. It worked, and my brothers Jack and Horace walked down to the station to meet me.

Somehow, we missed one another. Alighting from the train, I couldn't see anyone I knew, so I walked out of the station, loaded my kitbag rifle *etc.* into a taxi and headed to 25 Shrewsbury Road, where my parents, brother Tom, and sister May welcomed me with open arms. It was about half an hour later when Jack and Horace returned thinking I hadn't been able to make it. I don't think I have ever had so many hugs, kisses and handshakes and pats on the backs in my life. I cannot express my feelings as I entered the house. It was all too strange and wonderful to be home again.

After another thirty minutes of talking, Jack and Horace left so I could get to bed. I was exhausted and bed called me. Next day, Sunday, it was more questions and answers. They couldn't get over how well and fit and tanned I looked.

Monday saw me back at the railway station bound for York. Here I handed in all equipment except the battle dress I stood up in and my boots. I was given a choice. I could either have a blue pin-striped suit or a sports jacket and flannels, a shirt, underwear, socks, tie, 40 clothing coupons and a small suitcase. Because I had to take the suit to a tailor for alterations, I had to walk around in my uniform for a week. Believe it or not, that suit and sports jacket and flannels was my complete wardrobe for a whole year. And so, dear reader, after receiving a railway ticket for the return journey to Stafford, and one last request to "Sign here," I walked smartly out of the Centre.

The great adventure was over, and so on 13 April 1947, Sergeant Gilbert 524 of the Royal Regiment of Artillery was once again plain Mr. Vincent F. Gilbert.

About the Author

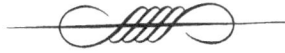

Vinnie Gilbert was born in Stafford, England in 1925 and received an education at St. Patrick's Elementary School and the College of Technology in that same town. In World War II he was enlisted into the Royal Regiment of Artillery at the age of 18 and served in India. He immigrated to Canada in 1965 and now lives in Guelph, Ontario.

www.ingramcontent.com/pod-product-compliance
Lightning Source LLC
LaVergne TN
LVHW011349080426
835511LV00005B/218